Pursuing a Successful Mindset

22 Attributes That Every Aspiring
Or Current Entrepreneur Must Master
In Order To Achieve Success!

By: Alfred E. Drum

PURSUING A SUCCESSFUL MINDSET

Copyright © 2020 Alfred E. Drum

1405 SW 6th Avenue • Ocala, Florida 34471 • Phone 352-622-1825 • Fax 352-622-1875
Website: www.atlantic-pub.com • Email: sales@atlantic-pub.com
SAN Number: 268-1250

No part of this publication may be reproduced, stored in a retrieval system, or transmitted in any form or by any means, electronic, mechanical, photocopying, recording, scanning, or otherwise, except as permitted under Section 107 or 108 of the 1976 United States Copyright Act, without the prior written permission of the Publisher. Requests to the Publisher for permission should be sent to Atlantic Publishing Group, Inc., 1405 SW 6th Avenue, Ocala, Florida 34471.

Library of Congress Control Number: 2020905524

LIMIT OF LIABILITY/DISCLAIMER OF WARRANTY: The publisher and the author make no representations or warranties with respect to the accuracy or completeness of the contents of this work and specifically disclaim all warranties, including without limitation warranties of fitness for a particular purpose. No warranty may be created or extended by sales or promotional materials. The advice and strategies contained herein may not be suitable for every situation. This work is sold with the understanding that the publisher is not engaged in rendering legal, accounting, or other professional services. If professional assistance is required, the services of a competent professional should be sought. Neither the publisher nor the author shall be liable for damages arising herefrom. The fact that an organization or Web site is referred to in this work as a citation and/or a potential source of further information does not mean that the author or the publisher endorses the information the organization or Web site may provide or recommendations it may make. Further, readers should be aware that Internet Web sites listed in this work may have changed or disappeared between when this work was written and when it is read.

TRADEMARK DISCLAIMER: All trademarks, trade names, or logos mentioned or used are the property of their respective owners and are used only to directly describe the products being provided. Every effort has been made to properly capitalize, punctuate, identify, and attribute trademarks and trade names to their respective owners, including the use of ® and ™ wherever possible and practical. Atlantic Publishing Group, Inc. is not a partner, affiliate, or licensee with the holders of said trademarks.

Printed in the United States

PROJECT MANAGER: Kassandra White
INTERIOR LAYOUT AND JACKET DESIGN: Nicole Sturk

AUTHOR BIO

I GREW UP ON a small cattle ranch in Northern California where I learned the importance of hard work and self-motivation. I also grew up in a very religious, yet economically modest, home where I was taught not only integrity and moral cleanliness but also how to be thrifty and conservative with money. As a youth and young adult, I received many opportunities to be a leader and to invest my own money, mostly in the cattle business because that was what I knew growing up. But when I failed to make it financially in the cattle business, I had to let go of some of my old ways of thinking, be willing to try new things, and open my mind to other business ideas and opportunities. That's when I was introduced into the world of real estate investing, a world which I knew very little of at the time. About the time I got out of the cattle business and was forced to get a regular job, we had the real estate crash of 2008, and, suddenly, single family housing was very affordable, and foreclosures opened the door for anyone looking to invest money in real estate to get some fantastic deals. I was lucky enough to eventually jump at the opportunity myself, and through a lot of study and trial and error, I was able to build a very successful business in just nine years. I started with very little but was able to leverage myself through intelligent loans and effective partnerships that helped me to build a successful real estate business in a short period of time. But it was my past experiences and the mindset I had to learn to develop overtime that prepared me to have the ability to see an opportunity and make the most of it. At the age of 36, I currently own over a dozen multifamily properties, which include apartments and trailer parks, and continue to flip seven or eight single-family homes per year. I am married with three children, currently living in the area where I grew up, and am very active in my church and local community. I hope to continue building my real estate business for years to come, but I also desire to be an inspiration to others looking to better their own lives by teaching them through my writings. I feel it is my obligation to pass on what I have learned to the rising generation or anyone looking to be successful in their own life or business pursuits.

TABLE OF CONTENTS

INTRODUCTION: A Successful Mindset..1

CHAPTER 1: Have Vision 5

CHAPTER 2: Maintain a Positive Attitude...11

CHAPTER 3: Be Teachable 19

CHAPTER 4: Exercise Self Control..27

CHAPTER 5: Have the Courage to Take Risks..................................35

CHAPTER 6: Become Self-Motivated 43

CHAPTER 7: Be Determined 51

CHAPTER 8: Obtain a Great Work Ethic...61

CHAPTER 9: Be Decisive 71

CHAPTER 10: Stay Organized...79

CHAPTER 11: Develop People Skills...89

CHAPTER 12: Aspire to Be a Good Leader 101

CHAPTER 13: Become a Problem Solver...109

CHAPTER 14: Learn How to Analyze 119

CHAPTER 15: Develop the Ability to Negotiate 127

CHAPTER 16: Figure Out How to Leverage Yourself 137

CHAPTER 17: Develop Patience 147

CHAPTER 18: Become Flexible 155

CHAPTER 19: Learn Accountability 165

CHAPTER 20: Be Focused 175

CHAPTER 21: Show Integrity 183

CHAPTER 22: Learn Humility 191

CONCLUSION 199

INTRODUCTION

A Successful Mindset

WE LIVE IN A WORLD full of knowledge, wonder, and opportunity—especially those of us who have been blessed to live in this day and age and in the United Stated of America. This truly is a great time to be alive, and this country truly is the land of opportunity.

We also no longer live in an era once known as the "Industrial Age," but rather, we are in a new modern era, known as the "Information Age." Technology now floods the Earth, giving us information and communication more rapidly and on a larger scale than ever before, and we are all blessed to participate if we so choose.

There has also never been a greater time to be an entrepreneur and start your own business or company. Financial opportunity is pretty much everywhere you look if you have the eyes to see it. So, what exactly is an entrepreneur? We mention the word quite often without stopping to wonder what it really means. According to the online dictionary "Investopedia," an entrepreneur is "a person who starts a business and is willing to risk loss in order to make money." Another definition I've heard for the word entrepreneur is "someone who solves a problem for a profit."

So now that you know the true definition of what an entrepreneur is, do you know who falls into this category or description? Maybe, this person describes you to some degree or another. Perhaps, this is who you want to be, but you're unsure if it's meant to be or not. Or maybe—just maybe—you're already on the path to breaking away from the pack and starting up your own business, but you are struggling to discover what you define as success.

Have you ever wondered what truly separates the mediocre businessperson from a truly great one? Have you asked, what is the difference between those, who are leading the way in their chosen industry, making plenty of money, and continuously growing their business, and countless others who are failing? Or, have you asked, how did these entrepreneurs setup their business into a system that pretty much works automatically whether they choose to jump in and participate or not, and create such a successful system? Did you think to yourself, how could someone build a business or a company, then step away and retire pretty much any time they feel like it without compromising their quality of life, and get to this point?

If you have asked these questions and if the entrepreneurs in these questions are who you aspire to be, then this is the book for you. But even if you just want to learn to live a happier and more fulfilled life, this book is for you as well. This book is truly about learning to change your mindset in order to achieve the level of success you desire to have in your life and to help you become the best version of yourself. We all have a champion deep down inside just waiting for us to unleash and therefore reach our true potential; the catch is figuring out who we are first, then learning the process of how to bring that person out.

We all have the potential to be great, and we all have the ability to reach our potential, but for some reason, most seem to fall short. I want to take you through my own personal journey of what I had to do to become a successful real estate investor with two separate money making real estate entities that for the most part run themselves. My wife and I manage them, but they produce financial results in such a way that we don't have to run around trying to do everything ourselves. We were able to create a system that does most of the hands-on work for us.

More importantly, I want to take you through my own personal business journey of how I had to learn and change my mindset—from a scared young individual with no clue of what I wanted to be in life to a successful real estate investor and entrepreneur with a crystal clear vision of my future. By no means am I saying that I am exactly where I want to be in my business or personal life or that I have all the answers. I still have many goals I want to accomplish and many more dreams I would like to see fulfilled. It's important to never be satisfied and to always be striving for better. I do feel that my story and personal experience of how I found success as an entrepreneur can be used as a great teaching tool for others on a similar path—people who are aspiring to not only become successful in business, but also successful in life.

The reason I titled this book *Pursuing a Successful Mindset* is because achieving a winning mindset is a lifelong pursuit. It is a "process," if you will, of literally changing the way you think and changing how you view yourself. You see, we are naturally all self-satisfying and instinctive creatures whose natural tendency is to simply survive and adapt to our surroundings. But what if our surroundings are negative and self-destructive? How, then, are we to become the truly best version of ourselves? We have to find a way to break free from our prison of a destructive way of thinking and discover a higher way of thinking. We must discover a way that will get us to where we really want to be: living the life we desire to live and becoming the person we aspire to become.

One thing that every truly successful self-made entrepreneur has in common is a self-compiled list of attributes they had to mentally master in order to help them develop a winning mindset. So what I've done is taken the time to carefully lay out 22 positive attributes that were all key to helping me to start and build a profitable real estate business, and even more importantly, they helped me to develop a successful mindset. I have put these attributes in the order of how I had to learn and develop them, so that I could transform myself into the person I've needed to in order to become successful. I expect the continual development of these qualities to be a lifelong pursuit and process. This transformation process of the mind is not something you can make happen overnight, but rather, it takes months or even years of practice to overcome bad habits and replace them with good habits that produce positive results. So come with me on this journey into the mind of a successful entrepreneur and learn from my experiences of what it took for me to achieve success in my own life and business. My hope is that you, too, can discover who you are meant to be and find the courage to become that person.

Come on. Let us begin!

CHAPTER 1

Have Vision

EVERY ACTION WE TAKE in life and every task or project we fulfill always starts out as an idea in our mind that eventually leads to physical action. As human beings, this is how we are physically and mentally hardwired.

We live in a world full of constant motion and change, thus presenting us with countless options on how we fit into the picture. As individual beings, we are born with five physical senses on how we can process the world in which we live; these senses are sight, sound, touch, smell, and taste. Each one of these very complex senses are continuously and naturally streaming a network of signals to our brain, which is basically our body's command center, and telling it what we are encountering at the present moment. Our brain then processes the new information given to it by one, two, or all five of these interconnected physical senses our body possesses; then the brain analyzes this information to generate the counter response.

There are many variances that can influence how our brain responds to information that's given. We respond to stimuli differently based on factors such as where or how we were raised, the people we surround ourselves with, life experiences we have had, personality traits we were born with, or even good old-fashioned genetics. Regardless of these factors, our brain is programed to analyze presented information; then it comes up with a physical response of some sort that is delivered to the rest of our body before being carried out as an action that will satisfy or benefit our entire being. This is the scientific way our minds work, pertaining to how our thoughts lead to action.

So what does all this have to do with developing the mind of a successful entrepreneur? It's simple; as I mentioned earlier, every action starts with a thought. Where does that thought come from? Well, from our brain, of course! As a successful real estate investor and entrepreneur, I have come to learn that every single successful experiment, presentation, invention, project, or business started out as one tiny thought. One thought that led to another, then another, until it finally projected into a vivid story in our minds, where it is now possible to bring to life what is building up in your mind, converting that idea into physical action. But it all starts with an idea or a thought.

As entrepreneurs, we all call this idea "vision." It is inspiration, if you will, for the things we want to do, the life we would like to live, and ultimately, the kind of person we want to be. I grew up on a small ranch in Northern California where I was given the opportunity to learn the value of hard work and investing. My grandfather had retired after 37 years of 12-16 hour days as a dedicated truck driver. My father had just finished his schooling to become an elementary school teacher. We always lived next door to my grandparents, so when they made the decision to move away from the city, go further north, and retire on my grandfather's dream ranch, my parents decided to follow. So after months of searching, they found the perfect piece of property. It was a place where my hardworking grandpa could stay busy in retirement and a place where my parents could safely raise us kids in the country. Little did I know then, at only 8 years of age, that this little 150-acre cattle ranch would prove to be a training ground for me to develop my mind into the financially successful entrepreneur I have been fortunate enough to become today.

At that time, it felt as if I had died and went to little boy outdoor heaven! I loved the country life, and I loved being outside. I would spend hours lost on that ranch in my own little happy world. I had quite the imagination. I think my entire family or anyone who knew me could attest to that.

But it wasn't always fun and games. As I got a little older, my grandpa began putting me to work. Unlike a lot of kids I knew growing up, I actually enjoyed working, and I definitely didn't mind getting my hands dirty. I would help him with feeding cows, building fences, irrigating, hauling hay, and herding cows. I even got to do tractor work as I got older. The point I'm making is that there was always plenty of work to do, and I was always expected to help out. I always felt bad for kids who grew up in the city and did not get to experience farm life. Those early years working on the ranch with my grandfather and my dad were pivotal in helping me to develop a good work ethic, among many other positive character traits I was able to acquire. Apart from helping out with the chores, I was afforded the opportunity to purchase my own cows with money I had saved up, and then sell them later for a small profit. Looking back now, I realize how little I actually made, but at the time, it meant the world to me. After selling my first couple cows, I was taught that if I turned around and bought more than I had sold with my profits—rather than spend it all on toys that I didn't need—I could actually grow my money year after year. So that's what I did. I would take whatever small earnings and profits I made and reinvest it, so my next payday would be bigger than my previous one. As a young boy and teenager, I was not only developing a good work ethic, but I was also learning how to grow my money. I guess you can say that for me at that time in my life it was Investing 101.

As I grew into a young adult, my plan was to go to college, get a degree, and start a career. The problem was, I really had no clue what I wanted to do for a career and what I would study in college. After serving a mission for my church, I started back up with buying and selling feeder calves like I did when I was a teen. I also signed up for a few local junior college classes, having no clue which direction I wanted to go. However, as I started really getting into buying and selling cattle on the ranch where I grew up, something inside of me started clicking, and I fell in love with investing. I wasn't always making a ton of money, but at the time, I didn't need much, and I loved what I did. Most importantly I loved the idea of being my own boss and investing for a living. I would spend hours upon hours late at night in my room punching numbers on a calculator and coming up with business plans for my desired cattle business in my mind.

So what is the point I'm making with all this? The point is that for the first time in my young life I had a plan of what I saw myself doing with my life. I had a vision. I knew right then and there that a college degree was no longer a desire of mine because I did not want to work for someone else. I wanted to own my own business and be my own boss. Besides, I really struggled with school, so for me I did not see the point of spending all that time, effort, and money to earn a degree I probably wasn't going to use. Plus, I had always learned best outside the classroom in real life situations. For us as business owners, we call this the "school of hard knocks." This was who I was, and I think I finally started to accept this at that time.

I was in and out of college for a couple of years, but ultimately, I ended up dropping out in pursuit of the life I truly wanted. The life of an entrepreneur!

CHAPTER 1: Have Vision

It started with a vision: a vision of who I truly was deep inside and a vision of what I wanted to do with my life. You see, I have come to discover in my years of investing that becoming an entrepreneur is not just a career choice. It is a lifestyle choice, a way of being. It ultimately becomes who you are, which to me is to be an independent thinker and leader. This world, in my opinion, has enough followers; it needs more leaders and independent thinkers.

Little did I know at this time of my self-discovery, but the cattle business would not pan out for me, but it would be the springboard that would ultimately lead to my successful real estate investing business; it all started with an idea in my mind that grew and grew until it became a vision.

Just take a look at the modern world in which we live today. Can you imagine how most people from 200 years ago would react if they got a glimpse of what the world has evolved into today compared to what it looked like back then? We have buildings that reach upwards of 2,000 feet, vehicles and air planes that can transport us at remarkable speeds, images and sounds traveling at the speed of light accessed by anyone in the world at the push of a button, endless information at our fingertips through the internet, a medical solution to just about every disease you can think of, and home comforts mankind has never before dreamed of having. How did a world that's been around for so long suddenly change so dramatically in such a short amount of time? How did all of these remarkable creations and inventions come about in these last couple hundred years? I believe it's a result of mankind's vision for a better world and a more advanced society. But how do you think it all began? Just like anything else, it all started with a dream. In other words, a vision of what could be or at least what was possible. That's how everything starts.

Like I was describing in the beginning of this chapter, the mind is a powerful tool that we have been given. The mind can determine how far we go in this life and what we are able to accomplish as members of a complex society. We can let it take us down or use it to give us a vision of who we can be, and, ultimately, our mental state of being can empower us to be the best version of ourselves. But it all starts with having a vision of who we are and what we want to become.

NOTES

CHAPTER 2

Maintain a Positive Attitude

THERE ARE TWO WAYS we can look at life and every situation it presents to us: we can respond in a positive, constructive manner, or we can respond in a negative, self-destructive way. This is one of the beauties of this life; the choice is ours and ours alone. After all, this is our life, and we are the ones who get to decide what we do with it and, more importantly, how we live it.

So, with that being said, how do you want to live your life? Do you want to be known as someone who complains about every little thing, portraying negativity everywhere you go, or would you rather be known for having a positive outlook on life, spreading good vibes everywhere you go? I can tell you from personal experience that people who complain all the time and are pessimistic about every little thing never appear to be happy and are also not fun to be around. We all have problems, and life more often than not is unfair, at least from our point of view, but I believe that is all part of the plan each of us voluntarily signed up for. You see, I was taught in my church from a young age to believe that we all existed before we came into this world and that before coming down here we each agreed to take on and participate in the challenges this life or world would present to us. But regardless of what you believe, the undeniable fact is that life is unpredictable and does not always play out how we would like. In other words, life is challenging and can throw trials our way, and many times, we are never quite ready for it. But this is the world we live in, and I believe we were meant to make the most of it. Unfortunately, many of us do not. It all goes back to our personal mindset, how we choose to live our lives, and how we choose to respond to the things we cannot control.

Your mindset is everything! You can either be happy, or you can allow circumstance to affect you and choose to be miserable. I'm not sure that most people realize they actually have a choice between these two states of being: happiness or misery. I believe that everyone wants to be happy, but due to uncontrollable circumstances we oftentimes find ourselves in, we convince ourselves that fate has decided that we are destined to be miserable. But each and every one of us has within ourselves the power to re-write and define our own story, regardless of what our circumstance in this life may be. It doesn't matter so much how you were raised or where you were born in this world, because at the end of the day this is your life and nobody can take away your ability to decide how you want to live it or choose to be the kind of person you desire to become. If you want to be happy and successful in whatever way you define success, that is your right as a human being. I believe each and every single one of us has the potential to be something great and has the right to be happy, but it all starts with a positive mindset. You need to have a belief in yourself to become the person you truly desire to be.

I have to admit that there was a time when I had lost belief in myself and my ability to be both happy and successful, at least according to the standards I had set for myself. Growing up in a home where religion was the very center of my life always attached a flood of high expectation wherever I went. I still to this day attribute all of my own personal success and happiness to the way I was raised, but there have been times when high expectations definitely got the best of me. In my home, love for God and others were of a top priority, and integrity was everything. I was always taught that kindness, honesty, love of family, and life with a divine purpose were some of the major keys to my personal happiness, and this belief system has proven itself to be a major factor in who I am today. But growing up in the ideal Christian home wasn't always a walk in the park. Through absolutely no fault of my parents or anyone who took part in raising me to have high standards, I was imprinted with high expectations from the time I was very young. In my home, education and hard work were considered a very important part of life. Like I stated in the previous chapter, hard work always seemed to come somewhat naturally for me, but school was a bit of a different story. I'm not suggesting that I was one of those kids who hated being in a classroom and regularly skipped out on school work, but what I am saying is that school did not come easy for me, and learning in a classroom was definitely not my specialty. I consider myself to be a terrible test-taker, but my willingness to complete assignments and finish long projects got me through school without failing. As I got into high school, the personal struggles with school just got worse for me. Between juggling different teachers, schoolwork, social groups, peer pressure, and my journey to discover myself, there were times that I wanted more than anything to simply give up because of the pressure. I may have been a naturally hard worker and a kind-hearted person, but I was definitely not an academic scholar—not even close. I always felt quite fortunate to pull off a half-way decent grade in any of my classes, except for maybe P.E. I definitely had to put in the work, but the older I got, the more and more I realized that I was a "hands on learner," not a "sit in a classroom learner." I have always felt strongly that we all learn in different ways. Some learn best listening, others reading; I have always learned best by doing. Some need the classroom setting with a teacher or professor directing knowledge their way in the form of assignments and test-taking. For me, I have found that I best absorb information when I am giving myself projects and tasks to learn and accomplish. I am a self-motivated learner. I hate being told what to do and being force-fed knowledge. This is how I operate, and it's probably the reason why, when I got older, I wanted so badly to be an entrepreneur. But back then, I had no idea what I wanted to do for a career. All I knew at the time was that my family expected me to go to college, get a degree, and get a good job with benefits. I think that's what most every American middle-class parent wants for their child. That's definitely what was expected of me, even with my academic struggles I had in high school. When that time finally came, I dreaded the idea of school even more; I had no idea what I wanted out of school. College is a completely different mindset from high school, middle school, and elementary school. For one, you're there because you want to be, and two, you normally have to pay to be there. So, in my opinion, if you are going to pay for college, you had better have a purpose for being there. For me it was tough because I had fallen in love with the idea of working for myself, and that did not require a college degree. Plus, as I previously stated, I really struggled with school and simply could not see myself committing to several more years of learning in a classroom.

Being in and out of college for those three years or so was a huge hit towards my positive outlook on life and my self-esteem. I was definitely lost at that young adult stage of my life. It did not help at all that I was sent home early from my church mission in Houston, Texas, for clinical depression. I had struggled a bit in high school with depression, but it became much more evident and a bigger issue when I became a young adult, especially when I was away on my mission in Houston. Depression is different for everyone, but for me, it was a huge mental breakdown causing me to lose all focus, purpose, and self-worth. I would always explain it to others like a dark cloud that would clog up my OCD brain and scramble everything inside, leaving me to a point of physical and mental exhaustion. It was a serious trial for me at that time and even into the first few years of my marriage. I had tried some counseling and light medication, but I could not seem to find anything that actually worked. Over time though, between my fascination with figuring out how the mind works and even more specifically how my mind works, I started to learn what worked for me. I found some methods that helped me overcome that feeling when it would sweep over me, either due to life's challenges or due to moments of weakness. I discovered over time that when I started feeling that cloud of darkness come over me, rather than feed it with self-pity and negative thinking, I would give myself little tasks to accomplish and fight those negative feelings with positive re-enforcement. I trained my brain to let go of all the things I couldn't control and to start focusing on the few little things I could control.

You see, by nature I am a bit of an OCD control freak. In my opinion, that's part of what makes me a good business owner and leader. Unfortunately, it also presents a challenge for me when life doesn't go according to the nicely formulated plan I have in my mind. I like things to be in order, and by no fault of our own, that is not always how life goes. That's usually what the depression would do to me. It would take my orderly OCD brain and scramble it all up into knots, but once I started figuring out what was going on inside my mind and what it took to combat or dissolve those feelings, I was able to begin the process of overcoming my mental struggles. I also started accepting the fact that life is not perfect and neither are we. We all know that, but sometimes we have a hard time truly accepting it. I had to learn to let go of the things I couldn't control and accept that doing the best I could with what I had was enough. In other words, learn to go with the flow. Letting go of the things you cannot control is a difficult thing to learn, but it is key if you want to be happy and successful. It teaches you to have a positive attitude in any given situation and helps you move onto bigger and better things when you're stuck in a rut.

Training our brain to think positive thoughts when we live in a world full of negativity is no easy task. The brain is like any other muscle in our body in the sense that the more we exercise it, the stronger it gets. A strong brain can overcome any negative or self-destructive thought. It just takes practice and time.

As human beings, we are naturally engineered to gel with our surroundings, but what science and genetics don't tell us is that we also have the ability to beat the odds and decide for ourselves what type of people we become. It just takes years of practice to train your mind to produce positive thoughts despite all of the negativity being fed by society. It's called seeing our as glass half full, not half empty—being optimistic, not pessimistic. It's easier said than done, but it can be done, and nobody else can decide for you to do this except you. The key is "willpower."

For me another key to overcoming my depression and negative thinking came once I finally got a taste of financial success as an entrepreneur. A year into my marriage, I realized I was never going to make it in the cattle business, and I had to look at myself again in the mirror and figure out where I would go from there. I had no back-up plan, no college education to fall back on, and now a family to support. I took a caregiving job, which was not at all what I wanted, but it humbled me and at least paid the bills for the time being. It also gave me a lot of time to think about what I wanted to do next and gave me the time to study. About the time I sold all of my cattle and started this caregiving job, the real estate market crashed hard. Houses had tumbled down in price about half of what they were selling for only two or three years before. Even though I had never considered real estate or anything construction related, a huge opportunity had begun to present itself to me. While working my job, I began to really dig deep mentally and read every real estate and motivational book I could get my hands on. Even though I disliked school, I learned to love learning through reading other success stories and started to truly believe for the first time in my life that I had the potential to become a wealthy and successful entrepreneur. I became obsessed with learning and saving money. I had a goal in mind, and I became determined to reach that goal no matter what. I noticed that in all my reading of other success stories, positive thinking was preached again and again. It hit me like a ton of bricks. This was how I wanted to start thinking. This was how I wanted to be. I had to dig deep and learn to start changing my mindset to a more positive one. There were some failed attempts in my pursuit to make money in real estate investing, but because I started changing my mindset, I learned from these failures, kept at it, and successfully flipped my first house within a couple of years. Things pretty much took off from there—once I figured out what worked and what didn't.

The point I'm making with this story is, I was ready for this opportunity because I changed my mindset from "poor me, I'm such a failure" to "I can do anything I set my mind to." Everyone has to discover their own path to having a positive outlook on things pertaining to their own world, so that they can create their own version of success, whether it is success financially, personally, academically, or spiritually. It's all up to us to determine the kind of life we want to live and even more importantly the type of person we want to become.

Do we want to be positive thinkers and live happy, fulfilled lives? Or are we going to allow the challenges of this world get best of us by letting society and circumstance dictate how we think? Whether you are willing to admit it or not, the choice is truly up to you. Be positive, even if the deck is stacked against you, and you will be amazed at what you can overcome.

NOTES

CHAPTER 3

Be Teachable

ONE OF THE MOST difficult parts of growing up is realizing you don't know nearly as much as you thought you did when you were young. It's funny though because when we are first born, we're like dry sponges surrounded by pools of water, willing and ready to absorb any information that comes our way. It's actually been scientifically proven that we learn at a much faster rate our first few years of life than at any other time in our lives. That's probably the reason why children can learn a new language much easier than an adult.

So why do you think this is? After giving this subject some thought, I have come to realize that the reason children absorb information so much faster than adults is that they are teachable. They are still fairly new to the world, so they realize that there is a lot of information out there that they have not yet learned. Have you noticed that small children normally ask a lot of questions? This is because they are eager to learn, and also this is their way of admitting that there is a lot out there that they simply do not know. Babies learn at an even faster rate. Their brains are like a brand new dry sponge, easily soaking up large amounts of water every time they try, see, smell, taste, touch, or hear something new. The problem with sponges is that as they start to soak up water, if they don't regularly wring themselves dry, their ability to pick up more water really slows down or even stops completely. Likewise, if we get to a point in our life's journey to where we stop seeking out more knowledge or where we think we know enough, our ability to soak up more knowledge diminishes or dramatically slows down. Like the sponge, we must not allow ourselves to be stuck on past knowledge, but we must find a place to let it go and store it away, thus making room for new information to be absorbed. We may never get back to that brand new sponge that picked everything up so easily, but we can make a consistent effort to renew it somewhat by squeezing it dry to make room for more of life's knowledge. We will never know everything there is to know in this world, but I do believe that it is our mission in this life to never stop learning and never stop progressing.

So with all of that being said, are you still teachable? Are you still like that young infant or child that realizes there is so much to learn and is eager to discover new things? Or are you going to revert back to that teenager who thinks they know it all? Not to say that all teens are like this, but I do find it comical when your stereotypical, know-it-all, "I'm on top of the world" teenager suddenly finds him or herself cut off financially from mom and dad, having to face the harsh realities of life on their own for the first time. For most of us this is an eye-opening and very humbling experience. As you get older you start to realize that everything in this world comes with a price, and adulthood is not quite what you thought you knew it was. Most of us at some point in our lives will go through this transition where we thought we had it all figured out, only to discover we have no clue what we are doing. But that's okay. This transition can be scary, but this is how we reset our brains to continue absorbing more and more new information. It is good to be confident in our abilities and in ourselves so long as we don't get so prideful that we don't allow ourselves to be teachable.

Humility is the key when it comes to putting ourselves in prime position to learn new things; where on the other hand, pride can be detrimental to our progression as human beings. When we are too proud, we do not allow our brains to let go of past ideas and absorb new ones; we become stuck in the same place, never allowing ourselves the chance to learn and experience more of what life has to offer. In other words, pride can stop us from growing as a person—mentally and spiritually. Rather than hindering our learning, humility allows us to learn more. When we are humble, we are admitting that there is much out there that we do not know. Like the child or infant who realizes that the world is much bigger than he or she, we too must be willing to subject ourselves to a life of learning and experiencing new things.

So if being teachable is essential to progressing as human beings, then it is just as essential in helping us to become a successful entrepreneur or maybe even more so. Entrepreneurs have to be problem-solvers and need to be consistently learning new ways of overcoming obstacles to grow their business. Technology is always changing—so is our economy. Therefore, it is essential that we learn to change with it. It is essential that we learn to adapt to the ever-changing world in which we all live. Otherwise, we will be stuck in neutral, never moving forward and never living up to our true potential, because our old ways of thinking are standing in the way of embracing change and growth.

There were definitely times in my own life when I thought I knew more than I really did. It's different for everyone, but for me the occurrence of getting a little too proud or confident in life led to the sudden, humbling realization that I'm not as smart as I thought I was. This happened more than once. I have always considered myself to be more humble than proud, but everyone has their moment of weakness in this area, and I have had my fair share of these moments.

One time that stands out to me and that proved to be a valuable teaching experience was when I was starting out my feeder operation business of buying and selling cattle. I had it all planned out in my head; I was going to build up this successful cattle business, and I wouldn't have to work for anyone ever again and would make a decent living for my future family. I was so confident in my ability to accomplish this that I dropped out of college super early, never giving it a real chance. My mind was 100 percent set on being an entrepreneur, and nobody could convince me otherwise. I knew that I wasn't going to get rich in the cattle business, but I'd be doing what I wanted to and doing it on my own terms. Like a lot of young entrepreneurs starting out, there were many factors I hadn't considered before jumping in. Some of these were losing animals to disease or sickness, increasing cost of feed and fuel, and other miscellaneous expenses I hadn't counted on. Plus, I would get overly eager to chase good deals at the auctions, so I would buy lesser quality feeder calves or ones that were too young, and I would end up paying the price later for some of those poor choices. About three years into it, I started realizing that it wasn't working out quite like I had previously envisioned. Then I got married and had a family to support with a business that wasn't succeeding like I'd hoped it would. I did start up a side business to supplement the feeder operation, which was hauling livestock for other small ranchers, but there just wasn't a huge need for that service, so it was very part time. I even worked part-time as a laborer at the local livestock yard, which went against why I quit college in the first place, but sometimes you do what you have to do to take care of your family. After four years or so of trying to make a living in the cattle business on my family's ranch, I had to make the very difficult decision to sell off pretty much everything I owned and pay off all of my debts while I still could. I was going backwards by the fourth year, and I knew I had to cut my losses while I was still a little bit ahead. I truly felt like a failure at that time. All of my plans of making it in the cattle business were dashed, and I could feel all of the voices from people closest to me in my life who told me it wouldn't work and that I should have stayed in college. I ended up having to really humble myself and take a full time job doing in-home care, which is not at all what I ever dreamed I'd end up doing. I failed at the only trade I ever really knew at that time in my life. I felt like the business world swallowed me up and spit me out. I had learned a painful, humbling lesson.

One day shortly after all this happened, I was sitting on the couch watching a commercial about some real estate program being offered in the wake of the real estate market crashing hard nationwide. The program turned out to be a scam after careful review, but it sparked something within me. All I ever knew, at that point, was agriculture, and real estate or construction had never before crossed my mind, but I felt like this was an opportunity I could not pass up. The more I thought about it, the more excited I got. Researching online, I saw how cheap some houses were priced at in certain parts of the country, so I performed more research at real estate auctions when I wasn't working. Just months after getting out of the cattle business, I was building up plans in my head of being a wealthy real estate investor. The problem was, I started bidding on properties before conducting adequate research on the business, and I ended up making a poor decision. Fortunately for me, it wasn't a very expensive mistake. I bought a cheap house in Flint, Michigan for $5,000. Living in California, that seemed like a steal, and I thought there was no way I could go wrong at that price. Before making the trip out to the property, I found out that the property was not worth even that. In fact, that very house we bought, along with all of the surrounding houses, was condemned by the city and was being bulldozed. I turned around and sold it on the same auction site I bought it from for $4,000. It was a minimal loss, but my wife had a hard time trusting me for a while after that rash investment decision. I felt like I'd failed again and had a hard time trusting myself as well.

The point I'm making by telling these two business failure stories is, sometimes in life or in business, we build ourselves up to a point to where we let our egos get the best of us. We ignore the advice of those around us, which is what I did, and take our own path without considering that we might be wrong. We can also plunge into financial decisions without doing the proper research or talking with those who are experts in the field, which is also what I did. Last of all, we expect everything to come easy and go just like we dreamed it all up in our head. I had big dreams, but I was not prepared for reality.

However, I refused to let those business failures keep me down, so I kept at it. This time I patiently studied everything I could about real estate investing, and eventually, I found success. I discovered the importance of investing close to home and learned how to properly flip a house through hard work and what we refer to in the real estate business as "sweat equity." This means that you are making improved physical changes to a structure or piece of property in order to increase its market value. It wasn't easy like I'd hoped it would be, but it was real. After I successfully flipped my first house with a trusted partner, I learned how to duplicate my success. I had to learn to put my own ego aside and start listening to the expert advice of those who knew more than I did at the time. This realization that I needed to be teachable was the breakthrough I needed in order to make it in the business world.

As young children, being teachable seems natural to us, but for some odd reason, most of us get more hardheaded as we get older, and we get stuck in our ways. We allow our own pride to keep us in neutral until someone or something intervenes and humbles us—hopefully reminding us that the only way we grow is to ask questions and take advice from those who know better. We need to reach out to those who have been where we are, tried what we are attempting, and either succeeded or failed in doing what we are trying to do ourselves. Learn as much as you can from others who already cleared the brush and paved the path to successfully do whatever it is that you want to do. Learn from their mistakes; don't pay the price and try to learn everything through personal experience. Although experience is arguably the best teacher, there are some negative experiences we are better off avoiding in life and in business. Learning from others, whether it is from their successes or their failures can sometimes save you years of heartache and failure. Pay close attention to all of the things they did right that ultimately led to their success, and then look at what they might have done wrong that caused them to go backwards or pay some sort of price, so you can avoid repeating some of the same mistakes. They obviously found some form of pattern or system that works in today's society, so figure out how you can emulate what they're doing and adapt it to fit your own pursuits. If it works, keep going and duplicate your success until you've reached your goals.

This sounds fairly simple because it is, but simple doesn't always mean easy. It takes time, practice, perseverance, and endurance to be successful in almost any business. These days there is a proven method to just about any business system you can think of. There is an old saying that goes, "Don't try to reinvent the wheel." If it's been done successfully by those who came before you, it can be done again. Maybe not exactly to the same level or extent, but if you follow proven patterns and stick with it, the same successful results can be yours as well. This is something I believe wholeheartedly because that is pretty much how I found success in real estate. I read all about others who succeeded in the very field I was pursuing and started listening to their good advice. It wasn't easy humbling myself to the point of changing my strategy and even my way of thinking, but it has been well worth it. I am a long way from where I aspire to be, because I keep raising the bar on myself, but I feel I am on the right track. We all need to find our own path, but don't be stubborn and learn the hard way. I am not saying to take the easy path because we grow through adversity, but you can learn from others. Be wise, don't allow yourself to plunge ahead and fall on your face if you don't need to. Be teachable, and never be afraid to admit when you don't know something or have an answer. Get in touch with your inner child and ask lots of questions. That is how we grow, and that is how we truly become the kind of person we've always dreamed we could be!

NOTES

CHAPTER 4

Exercise Self Control

We live in an impulse-driven society where we are bombarded daily with products and services that promise us instant satisfaction or claim to have the solution to our problems, whatever they may be. Every time you turn on the television, go online, listen to the radio, or drive down the street, it seems like there is some company trying their hardest to convince you that you need what they have. In other words, around every corner you turn, there is someone trying to sell you something.

With technology what it is today, there are many ways these companies can reach you with their flashy advertisements and promises. There has never been so many ways or opportunities to spend your hard earned money, especially with online shopping. These days, you can literally spend thousands of dollars with just the click of a button.

You also have credit card companies luring you in with the temptation to buy what you want now and pay for it later. This supports the idea that you don't have to wait if you really want something now because credit gives you the option of having it now and worrying about the consequence of paying it back later. This idea or concept also proves that we live in a very impatient society. These marketing companies will tell us things like "Live the American dream" or "You only live once." Credit cards or any type of credit for that matter literally give you the power to live above your means, and who doesn't want that?

Most of us are taught from a young age the importance of saving money and not wasting it on things you don't need. We are also taught that if you really want something and your parents are not willing to pay for it, you need to wait and save up until you have the money to buy it. So why is it that so many American middle class adults—no matter how much money they make—cannot seem to have any control over their spending habits? I believe the reason for this is when you don't have or make much money, you find yourself feeling somewhat deprived and thinking of all the wonderful things you could have if only you had funds to buy them. When money finally comes your way, you are mentally armed and ready to buy all of the things you wished you had when you were broke. Your mind can't wait to indulge into all of its past wants. Ever since the birth of the credit card this has been a huge problem in our country. Everyone wants to have it now and keep up with their neighbor. If you want that dream car or that fancy gadget that everyone else has, you no longer have to wait for it. With the swipe of a card or the push of the button, it's yours.

So how do we avoid falling into this trap? How can we save money or live below our means, when everything and everyone around us it seems is trying to get us to spend, spend, and spend some more? The answer is learning to exercise Self Control and training yourself to only do those things that will benefit you best in the long run. We are all human, and part of being human is, more often than not, tending to act on our physical impulses. For example, logically, we know that eating something healthy such as fruits and vegetables will help keep our body in good physical health, yet so often we give in to our bodies desires by eating things like chips and candy that we know are bad for our health. We do it anyways because that is what our body is craving. I call this the battle between what our mind knows is best for us versus what our body wants or craves, and we all face these types of dilemmas on a regular basis in some form or another. Fortunately, we are born into a world of laws, ethics, order, and expectation, which is how we survive and get along as an advanced civilization. In other words, in order to coexist with one another peacefully, we can't just do whatever we feel like doing. Our bodies, however, are born with the basic instinct to survive and self-satisfy, so from the time we are born, we are trained, by those who came before us, how to control our appetites and learn to adapt to our new surroundings. We are quickly taught that we can't always have everything we want, and if we want to get along with this world and others in it, we must learn to abide by its basic laws. Unfortunately, it is in our nature to satisfy our own desires with what I like to call instant gratification.

What does this mean? It means we do whatever we want when we want in order to achieve momentary satisfaction. As we age, we gain more and more independence, but with that independence can also come the license to live our lives the way we want—not how our parents want. Thus, we enter the true era of free will, at least for those of us who are fortunate enough to live in a wonderful country like the United States of America. Unfortunately, many of us abuse that free will by reverting back to our desire to self-satisfy through instant gratification. This can range from using addictive substances to having bad spending habits to becoming incredibly lazy. We all have fallen trap to one form of self-satisfying behavior or another at one point in our lives.

I believe we are put on this earth for many reasons; one of them is to learn lessons, such as mind over matter; in other words, we are here to learn self-control. This is a challenge we all face every waking second of our entire lives, whether we realize it or not. Every moment we are presented with many options, and it is up to us to decide what we do and how we do it. That is the beauty of free will. But we must always remember that while we are free to make our own choice, we are not free to choose the consequence that comes with making that choice. This is a basic universal law that we are all subject to, whether we like it or not. It's similar to the law of gravity; you are free to test it, but once you do, you are at its mercy, and gravity will always win.

One thing I've noticed about making poor choices is, in the beginning you have many options, but as time goes on, your options are lessened because you didn't make the necessary corrections. This basic principle applies to almost anything we do or don't do in life, especially when it comes to money habits.

Now, I would like to take you back to a time in my own life when I was taught some basic money habits that truly helped me to build a successful real estate company from scratch. Growing up on a small cattle ranch, not only was I taught the value of hard honest work, but I was also taught how to be wise with my money. I bought my first two calves with money I had saved up from chores when I was 11 years old. My grandpa told me that if I fed them properly and waited a whole year, then I could turn around and sell them for a profit, assuming their health would hold up. So, being the eager yet trusting boy that I was, I took his wise advice. I didn't make a ton of money, but I did make a profit, and I learned a valuable lesson. If I don't spend my hard-earned money on things that deteriorate in value but rather spend it on something that increases in value, I can actually increase my money; in other words, I can make my money grow. At a very young age, my eyes were opened to the world of investing. I realized that if I kept investing my money, rather than blow it all on things I didn't really need, I could multiply my little herd of two cows into a dozen or so. I was hooked! Little did I know then, or even in my early twenties when I attempted to buy and sell cattle for a living, the habits I learned of investing as a kid and young adult would eventually transfer over to my ability to buy and sell houses for a living.

Another very important money habit I was able to learn very early in my life was how to live on a budget. This came mostly from the good examples, my parents, that I was blessed to have as a child. My parents didn't make a whole lot of money working in the education system, but they knew how to save a portion of what they made, and they knew how to live on a budget. My sisters and I used to tease my parents about how overly thrifty they were most of the time, but looking back I realize just how grateful I am for the amazing examples they were to me about how to control spending money. They never spent more than they made and were not wasteful.

I have always respected other cultures who are very resourceful and don't waste money. I feel our country has taken its great prosperity for granted. We are by far one of the most wasteful societies this world has ever known. We don't always appreciate what we have, and we do not seem to value the principle of financial self-discipline. My parents were great examples to me of this, and I have greatly benefited from their good habits. But nothing teaches like experience! Fortunately for me, when I met my wife, she already knew how to live on a budget and save money. The true test came, like it does for most young couples, when we had to learn how to do this together while raising a family. I have to admit, that first year was tough for us financially, especially with my failing cattle business. I even remember times when our bank account showed negative. It wasn't easy, but we would always figure out how to pay bills and get our finances straightened out together. We definitely learned how to work as a team, and we were forced to only buy what we needed. By our second and third year of marriage, we still did not make very much money, but we always found a way to scratch and save a little here and a little there. We knew how much our bills of necessity were, and we were always very careful with our spending.

Anytime we received a tax refund or an unexpected bonus check, we would put it into our savings and leave it alone. For me, this money was precious because I had big plans to invest it in real estate when the time was right, so I treated it like little seedlings I was gathering up to one day plant in the right garden.

At that time in my life, I wanted so badly to quit my job and get back to being an entrepreneur that I was not going to jeopardize my future by spending my hard-earned savings on things I didn't need. I was willing to make all of the necessary sacrifices to put myself in position to succeed as a business man. I think that is another key part of learning financial self-control, the principle of sacrifice. I truly believe this is something every entrepreneur must learn in order to be financially successful. To sacrifice means to give up something good for something better, or to pass on temporary pleasure for a joy that lasts a lifetime.

Like I said earlier, this life is full of choices, and it is up to us to decide what we want to do with our own lives. Do we want to settle for average and be like the masses, or do we want to step out of our comfort zones and reach for the stars? In my opinion, this is what separates leaders from followers—the will to step up and be better than we were and the willingness to make the necessary sacrifices to get to where we want to go and be who we desire to be.

So what about you? What are you willing to sacrifice in order to accomplish what you want in life? It starts with a desire, but it is practicing self-control that is going to help you to climb that mountain of success. So what are you waiting for? Figure out what bad money habits are holding you back from being a successful entrepreneur and correct them today.

NOTES

CHAPTER 5

Have the Courage to Take Risks

I know a lot of people in this world who are perfectly content just living their lives as normal as possible, so they don't stand out or take any unnecessary risks. These are people who don't like taking chances or putting themselves in any vulnerable position where they might look bad or fail. They tend to take the easier route when the choice is placed before them and will shy away from anything that takes them outside of their comfort zone. For the most part, they allow fear to guide them and dictate what they do or don't do in life. Now, don't get me wrong, a little fear can keep you from harm's way, but too much fear can keep you from doing the things you've always wanted to do or living up to your true potential. In other words, too much fear can hold you down.

My intent is not to put down those who have shy personalities or simply don't like being in uncomfortable situations. I have always felt that we are who we are deep down inside, and we should never allow anyone to try and change that. But as I alluded to earlier, I believe that it is our divine mission in this life to try our hardest to be the best version of ourselves.

Some people are born with strong personalities that make them more of a natural risk-taker; others are born with more conservative personalities, making them a little more cautious. I myself happen to be naturally more conservative, and that is not a bad thing. This does not mean that I cannot develop myself into being a little bit more of a risk-taker and learn to step out of my comfort zone, not allowing fear to run my life. I know from my own experience and by watching others that anyone can learn to overcome their fears and truly learn to step outside of their comfort zone. Sometimes all it takes is the right opportunity and a little nudge from those whom we love and trust to get over that one thing that might be holding us back from doing what we really want.

With all of that being said, I know that every single one of us, born conservative or risk-taker, have some fear or many fears that are holding us back in one way or another. That is part of what makes us human. It is completely normal to have fears, but that doesn't mean we have to give in to them. I truly believe that we all have the power to overcome our fears and live the life we were always destined to live. You just have to make that choice. It's also important for you to realize that being afraid is perfectly normal and it is a big part of what makes us human; it is learning how to control that fear that is the key to overcoming it and becoming courageous rather than fearful.

I have always been taught that the opposite of fear is faith. Faith is taking a step into the unknown, not necessarily knowing for sure what the end result will be. In order to overcome our fears, we must be courageous and take a leap of faith. I know from personal experience that stepping out of your comfort zone can be scary, but it is well worth it.

So what are you waiting for? What is holding you back from taking a chance on life and being the person you truly want to be or doing what you really want to do?

When I was a young child, I had a fear of meeting new people and having to talk to them. Just ask my mom. When we were in public, I would always stand right next to her, sometimes holding on to her pants for dear life. Maybe it had something to do with being the first born, but whatever it was, I was very shy around strangers, and I did not like being away from my parents unless we were home. I remember my first day of kindergarten; the teacher, who was a very sweet lady, was reaching out for my hand, so I would let go of my dad's leg. It wasn't easy, but after some major convincing from both sides, I finally let go and reluctantly went with her into class. As time went by, I slowly but surely got a little more comfortable with being away from my parents and eventually got to the point where I could comfortably converse with my classmates and even my teacher.

My church was a huge help for me in overcoming my fears of socializing with new people, including the fear of public speaking. In my church, we are given the opportunity as youth to give talks and teach lessons. Growing up, this really helped me to overcome my shyness as I had many opportunities to speak in front of the classroom and even in front of the entire congregation. This is not an easy thing to do for anyone, especially for those of us who are a little on the shy side. They say that public speaking is one of the greatest fears in our society, but it was something that was expected of me, and it was something I started doing at a fairly young age. As I got older, I started getting more and more vocal and less and less shy. Part of this is because I was fortunate enough to have a ton of support around me and had the opportunities to face my fears until they eventually became obsolete.

After graduating from high school, I had the opportunity to serve a full time mission for my church. I would be sent away from my family and friends to preach the gospel in a place I've never been to and talk to people I didn't know. That, too, like my first day of school and the first time I gave a talk in church, was scary for me—especially being away from people I loved and a place I was familiar with. But it was also an opportunity for me to overcome my fears and step outside of my comfort zone. I was living with other missionaries I didn't know, and, with them, I was talking every day to people I had never met before. From that experience, I learned so much, and I actually became more confident in my ability to speak to others about serious matters. I cannot begin to express just how valuable learning to have serious discussions with people you don't know is, especially when it comes to making it in the business world.

The point I am trying to make by telling these personal experiences is that everyone has something fear related that is holding them back or keeping them from achieving their dreams. I don't know anyone who is 100 percent fearless. Whether we want to admit it or not, we all have something that we are afraid of. I think the reason that most of us do not like taking risks is because we are afraid of failure.

Risk-takers realize that there is always a chance of failure whenever they try something for the first time or make a business decision. The fact is, most small businesses fail within the first five years of doing business, and most ideas don't pan out the first time around. So what is the secret to succeeding? Unless you're just a very lucky person, most successful entrepreneurs fail multiple times before getting it right and discovering a winning formula that works for them. The secret is to never give up on your dreams and to not be afraid of failure. How do you think some of the greatest scientific discoveries of our time occurred? I'm sure any great scientist or inventor would tell you that it probably took them dozens, or even hundreds, of failed attempts before getting it right. But once they finally did, the world would never be the same. All of this is because of their relentless efforts.

Had it not been for their courage and willingness to think outside the box and take a risk, we would not have many of the comforts and luxuries that we enjoy today. I can't imagine a world as populated as ours without electricity, running water, vehicles, telephones, computers, satellites, internet, and medicines and vaccines for just about anything you can think of. We live in a wonderful time, where so many roads have been paved and discoveries have been made, but it's important to remember those who did the paving and who made the discoveries. It's even more important to figure out what character traits made them who they were and how we can have the same fearless mentality: the mentality of not being afraid of taking a risk, even if it means paving your own path and doing your own thing.

So many of us are too afraid, not only of failing, but also of what others might think if we decide to go against the crowd and be different. But different is good; that's what makes the world so interesting: the fact that we are each very unique and that there are people out there that aren't afraid to take chances and be leaders rather than followers. This world definitely needs more leaders, who are not worried about what others think and who do what is best rather than what is popular.

Going back to my earlier years when I was just getting into the cattle business, I can remember a specific time going to a livestock auction with my grandpa. We were sitting there on the hard bleachers, listening to the auctioneer, watching one feeder cow after another pass through the arena. We had been to the auction together many times, but this time was different. This time we were there with the intentions of him trying to help me officially get into the cattle business as an adult. To this day, I can remember my grandpa leaning in closer to me, nudging me, and telling me, "You need to start bidding on something, so you can get your feet wet." When I was a youth, he had always bought the calves, and I would then buy them from him. This time was different; this time he expected me to buy them myself and do my own bidding. If you've never participated in an auction before as a buyer, it can be a little intimidating. Here I was, this young guy just a couple years out of high school attempting to bid against mature cowboys who had been doing this for many years. It was scary, but I knew why I was there, and I couldn't let fear stop me from starting my business. I started putting my hand up when a feeder came through that fit my buying criteria. Being young and being the new guy, I had to shake my hand somewhat aggressively to get the auctioneer's attention every time I put up my hand. I was outbid most of the time, but I hung in there with my grandpa by my side and was able to purchase several feeder calves that day. I can't begin to express how good it felt to do that with him there. I could feel how proud he was of me, and, more importantly, I remember how proud I was of myself for overcoming my fear of bidding against older, much more experienced buyers and for walking out with what I went there for in the first place. It felt great, and I wanted to do it again.

The more I did it, the better I got and the more confident I became as a buyer. Buying cattle at an auction was definitely a risk, but it helped develop me into the savvy real estate investor I am today. Buying cattle at an auction mentally prepared me for buying and selling on a much larger scale—real estate. I learned how to make quick financial decisions and how to take calculated risks. If you'll notice, I added the word "calculated" to the word risk this time. There is a major difference between taking chances without doing any research on a subject and taking chances after having done your due diligence. It can be the difference between making thousands of dollars or losing thousands of dollars, especially in real estate. Buying and selling feeder cattle is risky, but it's not nearly as risky as buying and selling houses. With cattle, if you make a mistake, it can cost you hundreds. With houses, if you make a mistake, it can cost you thousands, sometimes tens of thousands. Hopefully my experiences can give you an insight into what it takes to overcome fear in your own life.

How are you going to overcome fear, so you, too, can learn to be not just a risk-taker, but a calculated–risk taker? Always make sure to do your fair share of studying and research on any field before you jump into it. At the end of the day, if you do not have what it takes to go for it, despite the fact that you might fail in your first or second attempt, all of that studying and researching doesn't really do you a whole lot of good. Nothing teaches like experience, but you have to take that leap of faith by taking action or nothing will happen. You don't want to miss an opportunity and always wonder "what if." Don't live your life with any regrets. You only get one shot at this life; don't let it go to waste.

So ask yourself this: am I going to stay in the slow lane where I know I can't get hurt or am I going let go of my fear and jump into the fast lane, where I might stumble at first but I will give myself a shot at living the life I've always dreamed of living? Let me tell you, driving in the fast lane of life is so worth it—if you have what it takes. You just have to learn to let go of your fears and take that chance. You have to be a risk-taker!

NOTES

CHAPTER 6

Become Self-Motivated

ONE OF THE THINGS I've noticed in my years as a business owner is that not everyone has what it takes to be an entrepreneur, and that's okay. In fact, our economy on a national or a global level would not survive if everyone, who was capable of working, was a business owner and not merely an employee. We need employees. Have you ever heard the phrase, "Too many chiefs and not enough Indians?" Just like everything in life, there has to be order and balance in the work place. You simply can't have everyone being the boss, and every business needs willing bodies to take orders from a higher authority, so that everything that's required to run that business can get accomplished.

Everyone has their place in this world, and just like the human body, every single part is important and vital to help it function properly as a whole. Employees are vital to every economy and business, big or small. I don't know what I would do without the people I have hired who help contribute their services to my real estate company. I know one thing for sure: I could not do it all myself, nor would I want to try. With all of that being said, this world does need more leaders, and more people willing to take charge. I'm not saying that being a follower is a bad thing. What I am trying to say is that there are too many folks who just want to show up, put in their time, go home when it's quitting time, and not have to think about their work until the next shift. There are also too many people who can't seem to get anything done on their own. They need someone to push them along and tell them every little thing that needs to be done, or they simply won't do it. They show up late, leave early, and have a hard time seeing jobs through on their own.

Now, I want to make it clear that I am not suggesting that every employee has this attitude or way of thinking. I know many employees who are self-motivated and don't need to be reminded or told every little thing in order to get a job done. But unfortunately, this negative behavior describes far too many adults who make up the working class in our country today. I think in many ways, government welfare programs, technology, and modern day comforts make us a little lazier as a society, and they discourage hard, honest work—or at least make it more difficult to achieve. The resulting problem is that so many of us lose sight of the priceless benefit that comes from hard work and ambition. There are too many jobs these days that can be done at the push of a button, and it is too easy to get a paycheck without having to work for it or produce anything useful.

That is why I believe that, in order to create a more productive and self-reliant society, it is vital that we as a people learn to be more self-motivated. For example, if everyone made the same amount of money, regardless of what their skill-set was or how much contribution they made to a company, what would be the motivation to do their best and work any longer than what's required? We would be constantly looking over our shoulders comparing our efforts to those who are only doing the bare minimum. Wouldn't it be safe to assume that we ourselves would want to lower our own standards by doing less, so that the pay would be fair across the board? An economy as complex as ours would never survive with a system that equally rewarded everyone the same no matter what their contribution was. We need the freedom to compete with one another and be rewarded for our efforts, skillsets, ideas, and results. That is what makes this country so special: the freedom to allow us to be whatever we want and go as far as we're willing to go.

The willingness to be a true leader and the ability to be self-motivated is, in many ways, one of the things that separates the successful entrepreneur from the mediocre one. For the most part, it is also what separates most employees from business owners. I believe that this, like many other character traits, isn't necessarily something we are born with, but rather it is something we must develop.

For the most part, I have always been fairly self-motivated, but like any other entrepreneur, I had to learn how to be self-motivated through personal experiences that gave me the opportunities to see jobs through without being pushed or told exactly what to do. I had to learn that if I saw something that needed to be done, I should push myself to do it, not sit around and wait for someone else to take action. One thing that I remember about myself as a child is that I hated a messy house, and I did not like things to be out of order. I guess you can say I was a little OCD. I would clean most of the house on a regular basis without being told because the mess would drive me crazy. I always preferred to clean when my mom wasn't around, so I could do it how I wanted. The only problem was that I was always getting in trouble when they couldn't find something because I either accidentally threw it away or couldn't remember where I put it. Other than that, though, my mom was always grateful I was willing to clean the house without being told. I had a very similar mindset whenever it came to my school work. I hated studying for tests and doing the day to day assignments, but when it came to long projects where we had the freedom to pick our own subject, I excelled. I always preferred to be given a project to do on my own terms versus being given a specific assignment that had to be done on someone else's terms. This was probably one of the main reasons why I did not care too much for school and why I struggled to excel in my studies. I enjoyed learning and had a great work ethic as a kid, but I wanted to do things my own way. I guess you can say I was kind of hardheaded as a kid, but I think most natural leaders start out that way.

I had many opportunities, working with my grandpa on the ranch, to develop myself even more into being a self-motivated person and an entrepreneur. In the very beginning, it was pretty much my grandpa telling me exactly what he wanted done, and him staying there to make sure I did it the way he wanted. Being the stubborn kid that I was, this sometimes would lead to fights, but at the end of the day, I would always end up doing things the way he wanted. By doing so, I started to gain his respect more and more as I got older.

Likewise, an important lesson I feel that we all need to learn in life is that in order to be a good leader, we must first learn to be a good follower and take the time to learn from those who know better. That is a lot easier said than done, especially for me, but I have really benefited from humbling myself in order to better lead others. Back to the ranch, slowly but surely, my grandpa started giving me more and more freedom to figure out by myself how to get jobs done without him shadowing me, which was not an easy thing for him, being the controlling person that he was. He is most likely the source from which I picked up my control issues. I think my grandpa always knew that in order for me to grow, eventually I had to learn to figure things out on my own. He could show me something a few times, but I couldn't really learn until I did it on my own. A great example of this was learning how to raise my own calves to make sure they got fed and were taken care of whenever they got sick. If I failed to do these things the right way, it would usually result in both the calf dying and me losing my hard-earned money. As I got older, I was expected to feed all of the cows in the winter, help irrigate in the summer, medicate any sick or infected cows, do tractor work, and help with all of the upkeep of the fencing. I was given much more responsibility as I proved myself throughout the years. If I slacked off or forgot to do something, it was my responsibility, and I had to accept the consequences. By my family entrusting me to help take care of the ranch and the cattle at a young age, I really developed the ability to become more self-motivated and act responsible enough to handle certain tasks without having to be told or pushed into doing them.

There is an old saying that I've always found to be very valuable as a leader: "You can give a man a fish and feed him for a day, or you can teach a man to fish and feed him for a lifetime." As leaders, if we don't take the time to teach others and give them the opportunity to learn from their own experience, then we are depriving them from having the chance to be leaders themselves. Without these opportunities, they will remain reliant upon others for their survival. We need more fishermen in our society, more independent thinkers who aren't so dependent on someone or something to take care of them and do the thinking for them. In other words, we need more leaders to step up and make things happen. But this cannot happen overnight—it takes time and experience, sometimes many years of experience.

This is one reason why I feel that we as leaders should learn to delegate responsibility to others, not only so we can get more done, but more importantly so that we can give others the opportunity to learn for themselves. I have seen many examples in my life of parents who do too much for their kids and simply don't take the time to teach them how to do things for themselves. Their kids wind up really struggling when they get out on their own. They think they're helping them by doing everything for them, but in reality they are crippling them because they are not teaching them how to be independent. I know from personal experience that sometimes it's easier to just do something yourself rather than try to explain it to someone else who doesn't know, but in the long run, they will be so much more grateful if you take the time to teach them. I think that is one of the solutions to the problem our country faces regarding being a more self-motivated society. Those of us who are currently in leadership position need to do more than just lead the way; we need to teach others to lead, giving them the same opportunities someone once gave to us.

On the flip side, if you are struggling to find the motivation and drive to be more than you are and do more than just the bare minimum, just know that anyone, regardless of who they are or where they come from, can learn to develop the ability to have that inner drive and ambition it takes to succeed in life. You just need to start looking for opportunities where you can complete little projects or tasks without anyone pushing you or pressuring you to do them. The key is to make sure you're doing and learning something you're passionate about. Then you must make certain that you finish whatever it is you've decided to start—in a timely manner. Do not procrastinate! Get it done, and you will feel so amazing that you accomplished something completely on your own. This alone can spark something inside of you that will make you want to do it again. It's called momentum, and don't let it go once you find it.

One challenge that can come from being overly self-motivated can be an unwillingness to allow others around you or who work with you to do what they do best and help you achieve whatever it is you are building or trying to accomplish. I have definitely fell victim to this way of thinking at times in my real estate business, as I grew up having to figure out how to do things all by myself on the ranch, but in my pursuit of learning to be more self-motivated it is also very important to be a team player. There are times when you need to rely on others it can't always be you leading the charge.

As I said earlier, I like things done in a certain way, and I hate relying on other people to do them for me, which is probably why I really struggled at first with hiring handymen and contractors to work on my projects. However, if I wanted my business to grow, I had to learn to let go of the reins a little and trust others to help me get the jobs done. Besides, I hated working on houses, and the contractors could do a much better job than I could. In business, some of the most memorable and valuable lessons come when our mistakes or lack of effort causes us to lose our own money, and I had my fair share of these types of lessons learned, but a lot of it came from trying to do too much myself rather than relying on others when the moment does call for it. That being said, being self-motivated is still very important in my real estate business.

This world is full of people who don't mind spending their whole lives living on someone else's terms and doing things someone else's way. However, this is not how a successful entrepreneur thinks. Entrepreneurs do things to the beat of their own drum. They don't need someone to motivate them to get anything done. They find it within themselves to do that on their own. They are self-motivated. So now that you know what it takes to break out from what I like to call "The Employee Mentality," what are you going to do to change your mindset? How are you going to get the point in your life where you become the captain of your own ship and the master of your own sea? Self-motivation comes from within, and it's up to you to bring it out in yourself!

NOTES

CHAPTER 7

Be Determined

ONE OF THE MAIN things that separates a successful person from a less successful person is determination. This especially applies to businesses. There are some business owners who don't stop until they find a way to overcome whatever obstacle is standing in their way, and there are others who back down or falter the moment things get difficult. These two attitudes can most certainly decide whether any start-up business survives or not—because there will always be problems no matter who you are or where you come from. I believe this statement can apply to all our lives, and it is something we all face from time to time.

Another way I define the word determination is to have a never-give-up-attitude. We live in a world full of problems, and much of the time we experience these problems through no fault of our own. Problems happen, and sometimes the only choice we have is whether we are going to deal with them or simply give up because of them. You can take the easy path in life, or you can persevere, which is never the easier way, but it is this path that leads to more fulfillment and long term success. It is also the path that leads to growth. As human beings, we normally tend to take the easier or less painful route when we can. We try to avoid problems by looking for an escape. The desire for escape, the easy way out, seems to be our natural response. It is truly what makes us human. Now, don't get me wrong, in a lot of cases, avoiding problems is a good thing, especially if it keeps us out of harm's way, but avoiding them in order to make our lives easier or safer can truly hold us back from living up to our true potential.

Another point to bring up about determination is that it doesn't mean just facing our problems but learning to see them through. Despite our natural fears, most of us are willing to face our challenges or at least approach them with caution, but many people seem to have difficulty seeing them through or finishing what they started. They start with the hope of coming out on the other end successful, but as reality sets in and as unforeseen obstacles suddenly get in their way, they start to doubt themselves and wonder if they have what it takes to get through it or stick with it. They also start to feel uncomfortable and wish that someone or something would intervene, so that they can have their comfort back.

Who doesn't like to be comfortable? Unfortunately, comfort keeps us from growing, and when we stop growing, our chances for achieving any kind of success in this world greatly diminish. I believe most everyone wants to be successful in life, but not everyone is willing cross that comfort zone line, doing whatever it takes to persevere and endure to the end. Life pushes them down or pulls a rug from under their feet, and they give up because that seems to be the easier choice to make. Giving up is always very tempting especially when things get uncomfortable for us or when things aren't going as planned. But I promise you that if you quit every time life gets hard, it will become a habit, and that is not a habit you want to get into.

Now, there are times when it is necessary to stop what you are doing and try something different or take a different approach. If something isn't working as planned or if we find out that it's not for us, it is perfectly okay to take a different road. Through this, we can make discoveries and learn new things. In fact, if something isn't working, it is essential that we accept that fact and try a different approach until we find what does work. If we don't do this, we can end up like the hamster on the wheel who finds him or herself running and running but never getting anywhere.

However, if we are quitting because it's too hard or because we are getting uncomfortable, we are sending a message to ourselves that we are too small or too weak to handle the situation at hand. We are creating a mentality that will set us up for a lifetime of running from our problems rather than learning to deal with them. I have to confess that giving up has always been a personal challenge for me, or at least, it really used to be. I have learned through my business endeavors how to hang in there when things don't go my way or when life gets difficult. I tell myself that the only choice I have is to keep pushing forward, even if it feels like I'm treading in mud. Eventually, things will work out in the end; they always do if I don't give up on the situation. By no means am I where I want to be, but in this area, I am much better at persevering than I used to be.

As a young kid, I was really into active sports, especially contact sports. I loved football, and when I turned 11, I begged my parents to sign me up so I could play. I had spent a lot of time playing catch with my dad in the previous years and thought that I was pretty good, so I went into my first day of practice feeling good about myself. I realized shortly into it, however, that I was probably not going to be a ball handler because I wasn't as fast as some of the other boys on the team. The coaches decided I was best suited as a defensive lineman instead. Despite my beliefs in my skills, there was a lot of competition at almost every position, and I felt like most of the kids there knew what they were doing more than I did. I also realized it was going to be much harder than I had anticipated, and I was not as good as I thought I was. I had a really hard time with memorizing plays and rotations, which may also have contributed to me being stuck me on defense. It truly was a reality check for me, but despite being outside of my comfort zone and not getting the position of ball handler that I was hoping for, I actually stuck with it that year and finished the season. I rode the bench as a backup defensive lineman, but it was my first year, and I was one of the younger boys on the team, so I accepted my role.

I went out for my second year of pop warner football, but this time I had a year of experience, so I knew what to expect. I was one of the older boys this time around, and I was also in better physical shape, which definitely helped my cause. I was off to a pretty good start with practice, and it looked like I had a good shot of playing in the games as a defensive lineman, but I started to lose the fire for it and got to the point to where I dreaded going to practice, as there was more expectation for me to practice with a purpose. Even though I did love the game of football, I started feeling the pressure of succeeding, and I did not like it. I would rather stay at home after school and do what I wanted, rather than slave away at practice. The feeling of quitting swelled up inside of me to the point to where I asked my dad if I could quit, and he told me it was my decision but not to regret it. So, I took advantage of my freedom to choose and decided to quit. It felt good at first not having to drag my butt to practice every afternoon and do all of those hard drills, running in the heat with football pads. As time went on, though, I started to have regrets for not sticking with it and finishing out the season like I did my first year.

I wondered how good I could have been if I didn't quit, so when I got to high school, I committed myself to taking up football again and went out for the freshman team. This time I had accepted my role as defensive lineman. I was pretty good that year, but I was never quite good enough to start. I finished the season though and tried out for the JV team my second year. This time, like before, I was in better shape and had another year of experience under my belt. My first few weeks of practice were great. I was playing with a lot of passion, making a lot of tackles, and the coach took notice. I actually got to start in our first game. I was stoked! I didn't play as well as I had hoped, but I was starting, and that was enough for me. For some reason, I was always better at practice than in the games, which probably had to do with added pressure. For the next couple of weeks, I started getting harassed by some of the guys on the team because I didn't swear or drink, and they said I tried too hard in practice. I always felt that they were jealous of me, but who knows why kids like to bully other kids. All I knew at the time was that it made me start to dislike football again, even though I actually liked the sport and was getting pretty good at it. My grades in school were starting to drop also because of harder classes that year, so I convinced myself once again that I needed to quit football to focus on my studies this time. I talked to the head coach, and I quit the team only three games into the season. Once again, I felt a lot of regret as time went on. I was improving, and I could have gotten really good by the end of the year, but I let all of the pressure and bullying get to me and sold myself short again by quitting.

We are creatures of habit, and once we start establishing particular behavioral traits, it becomes who we are and can be very difficult to reverse. Once we have committed an action, it becomes easier to follow a similar pattern—whether that is a good habit or a bad habit. When pressures of life get to us, we tend to revert back to what we have done in the past, and we do what makes us comfortable. This is the reason establishing good habits at a young age is so important. In my case, I had created the bad habit of quitting and finding excuses to justify my actions or lack thereof. By quitting football repeatedly, I was beginning to establish an escape route every time things got difficult, and it started getting tempting to quit every time I faced pressure or felt uncomfortable. In fact, I even dropped out of public school for the last quarter of my sophomore year and went to independent study because the pressure of high school was getting to me. But fortunately, I got really bored doing school work all by myself every day and made the decision, with the support of some good church friends, to go back to public school. I was pulling myself back out from my comfort zone to face my fears of high school.

Once I started my junior year, I started realizing that I needed to face one more fear; I needed to return to football for my senior year of high school. This was my last chance to play the sport I loved and prove to myself that I wasn't going to continue to be a quitter. That winter, I started working out every day and preparing myself for one last year of football as a member of the varsity team. I even went to football camp, which was quite the experience. To make a long story short, my last year of football was a bit of a roller coaster, but I finished out the entire season including three weeks of playoffs. I started some games but mostly came in off of the bench as a backup. I did have some impressive practices, which really helped to boost my confidence as a young man and helped me to get through a long season. Before graduation, all of the seniors were asked to leave a quote of our choice next to our senior pictures, and I chose a very short yet powerful and meaningful quote that kind of summed up my entire childhood football and school experiences. I wrote: "Never give up." School and football were a huge struggle for me growing up, but despite quitting on several occasions, I endured and finished on a positive note. Little did I know at the time, but the challenges I would face as a young adult with quitting would continue.

But it's important to note that just because we may have failed ourselves in the past by giving up too easily and we have developed a bad habit of quitting every time we hit a wall, does not mean we are destined to live the rest of our lives as a quitter. Just like you can teach yourself to develop bad habits, you can also train yourself to overcome those bad habits by facing them and overcoming them through hard work, consistency, and perseverance.

When it comes to overcoming the habit of giving up too easily, the key is learning to see things through until you've reached the finish line. Start with small things if you have to, then work your way up to the bigger things that are more impactful. Before you know it, you will become more

CHAPTER 7: Be Determined

successful than you ever could have imagined. Determination can see you through just about any type of challenge or road block this life can throw at you.

It took me many lessons before I was able to break through and overcome my own challenges with giving up. One year after high school, I went on a full time mission for my church that was supposed to last two years; however, due to my clinical depression, which I was diagnosed with while on my mission, I was sent home early on an honorable release. I was sent home after only having served seven months, rather than the full two years that was expected of me. Even though it was an honorable release, I still felt like a failure because I didn't finish out my two years like most every other missionary did. I had prepared for this event throughout all of my teenage years, and I felt like I let not only myself down, but also the younger boys in the church who looked up to me. I also felt like I let down my own family, and even more importantly God. Even though I did eventually learn to make peace with my early release, this seemed to fit the pattern of me once again having difficulties seeing things through from start to finish. I started college three different times while I was still trying to figure out my life, and I never once completed a single semester. It became easy to quit because I had done it before, and even though my mission experience was the result of something not entirely in my control, by not completing my two years as a missionary, I was drawn back to that mentality of when things get tough you can always bail and come back to your comfortable place. It definitely affected my confidence, and that affected me in college. Even though college was not really for me, the fact that I didn't even finish out a semester that I had started got me back into the quit when things get hard mode.

This was something I needed to change if I ever wanted to become successful. So, when I started my real estate career after having failed as a cattle rancher, I knew I had no choice this time but to succeed and not stop until I did. My family and entire future was dependent on me making it work. I had gotten to a point in my young life that I had to learn to overcome my bad habit of quitting and see something through. After my first failed attempt at real estate, believe me, I wanted to revert back to my old ways and quit, but this time something inside of me would not let me do that. I truly felt deep down inside that I had found my calling in life, and I had to make the decision to not let go of that dream, no matter how difficult things got and how daunting that climb would prove to be. So I kept studying and tried a different approach that actually worked.

Once I got a taste of success by making money on my first flip, I knew financial success was possible or at least within my grasp, and I kept going until I figured out a winning formula that worked for me. With over 60 flips in the last nine years, I can tell you from experience that every single one presented its fair share of problems, stresses, sleepless nights, and multiple reasons to give up. But I knew every time that there was a financial reward that awaited me, if I could just find a way to get through the remodeling stage and get through escrow. I can't count how many times I thought my real estate business was in jeopardy of going down the drain because of a difficult project or escrow. I just had to keep reminding myself that if I can just make it through this next stage and keep my eyes focused on the big picture, thinking positive thoughts along the way, everything would be fine in the end. And it has been!

I am nowhere near where I want to be, but this self-talk that got me through so many flips and real estate projects and has definitely proven to be true in my life. So what does it mean to be determined? It means never giving up, even if you feel in that moment that the world is working against you. Always remember that when you're in the middle of your own mess trying to get to where you want to be and things start to look hopeless, life is just testing you to see if you have it in you to take that next step—even if it seems impossible. Even if it seems the odds are against you and you're not sure you have what it takes to succeed, find that next gear and keep moving forward. I promise that if you do, someone or something will be there to help pull you through to the finish line.

I have always believed that the universe rewards us for showing it our best efforts in life and not giving up on our dreams. I also believe that if you are absolutely determined to accomplish something in your life or be the person you want to be, and you refuse to take no for an answer, there is no limit to what you can do or who you can be—other than the limits you put on yourself. Be the captain of your own ship and decide today that if there is something you want more than anything but it seems out of reach or impossible, that you will do everything in your power to make it come true. Most importantly, do not stop until you get there. These are the two keys to getting what you want in life: be persistent and never give up on yourself. Never let anyone ever convince you that you are not good enough or that you don't deserve something. For many years that is exactly what I did and it affected my self-esteem to the point where I no longer believed in myself or my abilities. It was when I decided to stop listening to those negative voices from the past and even present that I finally gave myself the chance to truly succeed in my career and life. You may not always have the power to control what goes on around you or what is standing in your way, but you always have the power to decide whether or not to keep going. That is truly what separates the successful entrepreneur from the unsuccessful one: the ability to face those challenges and obstacles that make you afraid, the willingness to go places that put you outside of your comfortable place, and the determination to never, ever give up on what you are doing until you've reach your goal—whatever that may be.

So, what do you want to accomplish in life? What is it that you want more than anything but aren't quite sure if you can get there? There is an old saying that goes, "How do you eat an elephant? One bite at a time." So take that first bite, or step, to wherever it is you want to end up, remembering that there will be forces out there trying to stop you but also remembering that your perseverance can get you through any problem or roadblock that is sure to get in your way. Don't stop until you get there. Be determined!

NOTES

CHAPTER 8

Obtain a Great Work Ethic

Most healthy and capable adults spend the vast majority of their waking hours doing some sort of work-related activity. Now when I say work related, I am not just referring to a job that earns you money, but I am also including any type of mental or physical activity where you are doing something productive. This could include personal errands, house chores, schooling, mentoring others, paying bills, or even planning out your day. It also includes the time we spend driving to and from work. Basically, it is anything that feels like an obligation in our life and takes us away from our leisure time, where we would do things we actually want to do, rather than doing what we feel we have to do.

I would estimate that the average working class adult probably spends approximately 12 to 13 hours per day doing productive activity. Since most people sleep around eight hours per day, that only leaves three to four each day for us to do something we consider to be leisure time. Now this is not taking into consideration days off work or vacations, but is referring to your average work day of the week. The bottom line is that nearly all of us will spend most of our lives doing some form of work. This seems to be one of our main purposes for being here on earth, to learn how to be productive members of the society in which we are living.

So if work is such an important part of our mortal existence, then why do most of us dread doing it or look for ways to avoid it? Probably because work, for most of us, is classified as a "have-to" not a "want-to" activity, and nobody likes being pushed into doing things they don't actually want to do. Now, there are some of you out there who are probably saying to yourselves, "I love what I do for work," and if that's the case, then you probably have already developed a great work ethic, just based off of the fact that life has blessed you with the opportunity to do what you want rather than what you have to do. I have known some people who really enjoy working and would rather be doing something productive than spending their time on leisure activity. This is not always because they get to do what they enjoy for work, but it's just the fact that they enjoy working. However, in my experience, I have found that these types of people are a rare breed, and society these days is producing less and less of them it seems.

But what exactly does it mean to have a great work ethic? I feel that one of the reasons why so many people in our society struggle with having a good solid work ethic is because their parents or leaders have not properly taught them how to work hard. Everything seems to come much easier these days, and it makes it very tempting to for us to always look for an easier, less painful way out or to seek out a less time consuming way to get something done. Or it could also be that many people growing up simply do not get enough opportunities to practice or experience hard work for themselves. That is one of the reasons I believe that it is vital for kids today to be given the opportunity to get as much hands-on work experience as possible in order to learn for themselves the importance of knowing how to work hard, rather than having things just handed to them. The lesson of learning to get what you earn in this world is priceless! So, what are some other things that might make it difficult for people to obtain great work ethics?

Well, a lot of it may have to do with the fact that modern day comforts and technology make life a little too easy and promote convenience rather than effort. What used to take weeks or even months can now be done in a day or less, and what used to require multiple people or physical exertion can, many times, be done at the push of a button. Society, over the last 200 years or so, has worked hard to discover ways of making our jobs and lives so much easier, that society in a way has made it too easy for most of us. I have often joked that if you were to take your average person from today and drop them off in the early 1800s, they would probably not last much longer than week or so. This is not completely true, because most of us are adaptable when we have to be, but you have to admit that most of us would find it very difficult if we had to deal with life back then, considering what we're accustomed to today. Between our smart phones, rapid transportation, medical options, and all of our in-home conveniences, we have it much easier compared to the days when none of these things existed and you had to travel several days or more just to pass a simple message.

Now, I am not suggesting that just because you are born into an advanced society like ours that you can't learn to become a hard worker, but what I am saying is that it does make it a little more challenging. Because most of us are blessed with modern day comforts and conveniences, we have to be much more self-motivated and self-driven in order to develop great work ethics in our lives. That is what this chapter is all about.

When I was younger and working on the ranch, I was given many opportunities to learn how to work with my hands and use physical exertion in order to accomplish the many tasks I was expected to do. My grandpa would line up chores for me to do each day, then go out there with me to make sure I did them the way he wanted. Now believe me, this was never a fun experience, being the independent spirit that I was, but it was absolutely necessary in order for me to develop the kind of work ethic I needed to be successful both on the ranch and later on in life.

You see, my grandpa was what you call a "workaholic," and I don't know if I ever knew anyone who enjoyed working nearly as much as that man did. He grew up living the farm life, and being the only boy, he was expected to help work to support the family. As an adult, he worked 37 years for the same trucking company, putting in an average of 60 hours per week. Finally, he chose to retire on a 150-acre cattle ranch so he could always stay busy working. He was a great example to me of what it meant to be a hard worker, and I always tried my hardest to live up to that example. So, even though I often times hated that he would shadow me during my ranch chores, he was not just watching me, but he actually took the time to teach me how to work and mentor me in order to help me learn to do the job right and help me to become a hard worker. In fact, unless it was a one-man job, he would be right there working alongside me. In the beginning, it was actually me being asked to jump in to help him out, but later, as I got older, he would expect me to take charge in doing the work on the ranch that needed to get done. Slowly over the years, I started to gain a better and better work ethic through experience and from the good examples I had before me, in my grandfather and parents.

It's always important to find examples of people who work hard and to use those examples as motivation to be a hard worker yourself. It's even more important to put your money where your mouth is, or at least practice what you what see, actually putting in the time and effort to learn how to develop yourself into a hard worker. This means not only putting in the time but being productive with the time you are putting in while always giving it your best, honest effort. You see, many times we can find ourselves just drifting through our work day, going through the motions, not really giving it our best effort, which, I suppose, is better than not showing up at all. But if we truly want to be the best version of ourselves and find success economically and professionally, then it is vital that we give it our all when we are working. Just like any other habit, if we do this on a regular basis, it will become who we are, and others will take notice. Most importantly, you will learn to enjoy working a little more because it will bring you self-satisfaction and that leads to true happiness.

I know for me I don't always enjoy working, and many times I dread going to do it. However, once I start accomplishing things and being productive, I feel powerful, and my self-worth goes through the roof. For me, personally, it has always been an antidote to my clinical depression, and I think it can have a similar effect on anyone who struggles in the same way.

So, what does it mean to have a great work ethic? To me, it means being self-motivated to work hard and learning to be productive while doing so. There is a saying that goes: "work harder, not smarter," but the truly successful entrepreneurs, in my opinion, work harder and smarter. They find unique and clever ways to get the job done easier or faster, but they also never underestimate the value of putting in the hard work. Just because we live in a day and age where you can do things at the push of a button does not mean we aren't afforded the opportunity to earn what we get through sweat and tears. I have always believed that the people who are most grateful in life are the ones who had to truly earn what they got. Nothing truly worthwhile in this life comes to us without having to pay some sort of price. If it's free, be careful—there is probably a catch. Some people do get lucky, but nobody's luck lasts forever. Eventually, reality hits us all, and if we don't put in the effort and make the necessary sacrifices, then we are decreasing our chances of holding onto our luck. Also, if we don't work hard, we deprive ourselves the opportunity for self-improvement because we aren't giving it our all and we are expecting things to go easy. Besides, if everything were easy, we would cease to grow and we would not appreciate success—or the world around us for that matter. We would become lazy if we expected everything to be convenient and come easy to us.

If you want to be a successful entrepreneur, you have to be willing to do what most aren't, and you have to put in the work. To put it in simple terms, you can't be lazy! This world could definitely use more people with great work ethics, more people who don't have to be told what to do and are willing to jump in and do what needs to be done because that is who they are.

When I started flipping houses, I found that each project had its own unique set of challenges, and if I didn't have the built in work ethic to persevere through each flip, I would probably not be a full-time real estate investor today or even an entrepreneur for that matter. I can't count how many times I wanted to give up or not show up to work at a house when I needed to, but like it or not, I knew that if I wanted to come out successful on the other end, I needed to do whatever it took to do to get that house finished and sold, so I could move on to the next project. I don't know if I ever had an easy flip, but there were definitely some that were harder than others. Every house flip I was a part of was stressful and caused me to lose sleep at night. To this day, that has not changed, but I feel like I am getting better at handling the stress of remodeling an entire house or apartment and I have the willingness to do whatever it takes, personally, to make sure it gets done.

I hate doing construction work even though I do love real estate itself, but it seems like no matter how big or small the remodel, I find myself diving in physically to help at the end on almost every single project I've ever overseen—just to make sure it gets done right. That way, I can sell it for the price that I need, when I need. For me, trying to finish an entire house remodel is the most stressful part of the whole process, but it's my job to see that the house is ready to put on the market. I believe, it is the work ethic that I gained working as a kid on the ranch that has gotten me through each flip and on to the next.

Another thing that I feel is important when discussing work ethic and entrepreneurship is finding out what your strengths or skillsets are and finding a career that best fits what you're good at, giving you the opportunity to do what you do best, whatever that might be. The other important thing is to find a career that you are passionate about. The way I've always looked at it is if you are going to spend a good portion of your life working for a living, you might as well make it something you actually enjoy doing. Why would anyone who wants to have a happy life choose to do something they hate or work at something that makes them miserable? That never made a whole lot of sense to me, but this is exactly what so many people do. They think it's too hard or out of reach to pursue what they want to do for a career, so they find themselves settling for the first thing that comes their way. Now there is nothing wrong with doing jobs that you dislike or that don't fit your personality—as a temporary stepping stone to get where you really want to be, so long as you don't get too consumed or comfortable, thereby choosing to give up on your dream career. If you are not doing what you love for a living and there is something you have always wanted to do for a career, don't give up on that dream, whatever it is. Be a fighter and don't ever stop working towards your goal. Once you achieve this, don't let it get away. You have to fight for what you want in this life, and believe me, if you don't, there will always be someone else there waiting to take your spot.

Another thing I want to note about work ethic is that even once you find your dream career, there will always be parts of the job that you will not enjoy. While, yes, it's easier to do well at something when you enjoy doing it and you're more apt to be successful, it is much more difficult to succeed when you have to do something you do not enjoy. That is why having a good work ethic is so important in order to be successful at anything in life. No matter what business or field you choose for yourself, there will always be that part of the job that you dread and that does not cater to your strong suits. You will have to deal with these things even when you'd rather not. This means that to have a great work ethic, you have to be determined—like we discussed in the previous chapter.

You cannot give up when the going gets tough or when you feel you haven't accomplished everything you should have. You have to push through and find a way to make something happen, even when the odds are stacked against you. You will be amazed at what you are capable of if you give it your best in everything you do and don't take the easy path, even if it looks tempting to do so. If you have what it takes to dig down and get through it, you will find that each time it will get a little easier for you to handle, and you will grow as an entrepreneur and individual. I am very grateful for the experiences in my own life that have helped me to develop the work ethic I have needed to get to where I am today, as a business man and real estate investor.

So figure out what you are good at, find something you are passionate about, and don't stop working at it till you get there. The process of working towards your goals will create a drive within you that will motivate you to give it your all in whatever you're doing and you will develop a great work ethic that will be there for you whenever you get to where it is you want to be career-wise. So buckle down and do your best wherever you are right now. Do this, and doors that you never thought could open will open for you and you'll be on the path to living the life you were always meant to live.

NOTES

CHAPTER 9

Be Decisive

LIFE IS ALL about making decisions and living with the results. Whether they are big or small, trivial or monumental, we make hundreds of decisions every single day of our lives. That is how we function as human beings, and that is how we accomplish things, even if that accomplishment is taking a shower or brushing your teeth. We are all born with free will and provided with a world full of options. We are able to process all of these options because we have been given a physical body with an active brain, which is constantly thinking and determining what to do and how to react to our surroundings and circumstance. Most of us take for granted just how powerful and highly complex our brains actually are. We also don't always realize how often we use them to make the day to day decisions. We can't even begin to process the number of decisions we make, but it is those decisions that make us who we are and determine where we end up in life.

When we start out as infants, we make a lot of our decisions based on primal instincts and basic needs, but as we get older, the decisions we make start to mean a little more to us and have more implications on who we will be and what we will do. In the beginning, especially when we are trying something new or different, we are very careful in our thought process on how we should proceed, but as we move forward with our choices, we begin to figure out what works best for us. These choices become habit-forming—or in other words, our new way of doing things. Now, while a lot of our minute to minute physical decision-making is based on instinct and natural reaction formed by previous developed habits, we are also consistently battling with ourselves on what we should do or say and how we should act or how we should respond to a situation that is affecting us somehow in the moment. A lot of the daily choices we make have very little impact on where we end up years from now or where those around us end up, but with that being said, I believe that many of them mean much more than we think they do at the time.

There is a saying I really like that goes, "Spiritual conversion is not a one-time event, but a lifetime of good decision-making and habits that lead to being spiritually converted." This is one of many things I was taught in church growing up, and it is a principle that I have found to be very true, not just in my own life but in the lives of those around me. It's not about making that one monumental choice that changes or alters your entire universe, but rather it is all of those tiny minute-to-minute, day-by-day decisions that create your habits and slowly determine who you are and where you are going. You can't build a house in one day; there are hundreds of specific steps you have to take in order for your home to be built right. If you skip some of these steps, you can have a serious problem when you go to move in. The same goes for ourselves and how we build our lives; if we think that the little in-between decisions don't make a difference and chose to only focus on the large matters when they come around, then we are taking our eyes off of the path that we are slowly heading down, and we will find ourselves skipping vital steps that are required to build the kind of life we truly want to have. Bottom line is that when it comes to making choices, which we all are required to do whether we like it or not, we cannot overlook the small decisions because those are the steps that can mold us into the type of people we become and will create the type of life we live.

So now that we understand the importance of making decisions in this life big or small, what does it mean to be decisive, and how can that help you to become a successful entrepreneur? Well, let me tell you from my own personal journey that being decisive is huge when it comes to running a business or anything in life for that matter. According to *Collins Dictionary*, the official definition for the word decisive is, "having or showing the ability to make decisions quickly and effectively." I can't count how many times I have had to be decisive in running and building a real estate investing business over the last nine years.

I have had to regularly make financial, property, and personnel decisions, some small but others not so small. For example, I have to decide if I want to purchase a particular property or not. If I do, then I must decide what exactly to do with that property once I have it. When a property hits the market or an auction, I don't always have the luxury of waiting weeks to make a decision on whether to pursue it or how much to pay, but if I don't do something, I may miss out on a wonderful opportunity. Many times I have had to act within the same day or within the same moment if I wanted a shot at buying a particular property the market presented me. Some decisions have made me thousands of dollars, while others have cost me thousands. Luckily, I have definitely made more good decisions than bad, but the point is, I made them and I didn't hesitate.

This reminds me of a saying that goes, "He who hesitates is lost." I interpret this to mean, if you spend too much time making up your mind, you will end up losing out on whatever it was you were trying to get or do. For my business, in an ever changing and competitive housing market, it is usually imperative that I make quick, smart decisions or else I have no chance of making any profit.

I have to admit that being decisive when it comes to money has always been a strong suit for me. But like a lot of other skills and attributes this is something I wasn't born with, it had to be developed over time. Going back to my younger adult years as a cattle investor, I had to learn how to be decisive when it came to buying cattle, especially since I only bought at live auctions. If you have ever been to a live auction, it can be an intimidating experience, especially if you are there with the intentions of buying—even more so if you are the least experienced bidder in the room. When I first started out, I fell into the "least experienced bidder" category. Thankfully, I had my grandfather by my side most of the time to support me and help me out, at least in the beginning. He would quite often throw hints my way on when I should bid and how high I should go, but I was always the one who had to do the bidding and make the final decision. For a young man this was a big deal and very empowering because my grandpa was allowing me to make my own financial decisions on the spot. I think he knew that in order for me to grow as a person and businessman I would have to make my own financial decisions, even if some of the decisions I made weren't the best.

But that is how you learn, not from someone else telling you what to do or how to do it, but from your own experience and mistakes. I'm not sure why but for some reason we tend to learn more from our mistakes than from our successes, so long as we don't let our mistakes defeat us and make us want to give up. This, again, goes back to perseverance; see how all these skills build on each other? I definitely made my fair share of mistakes when buying feeder calves, which usually resulted in losing money. However,

CHAPTER 9: Be Decisive

those were the lessons I remembered because I did not want to repeat my mistakes. I do not like losing money; in fact, I don't know anyone who does. I especially did not like losing money back then because I didn't have a lot to begin with, so every loss felt like a hit to my and my family's financial future.

Losing is definitely expected when you're investing for returns, especially when you're starting out like I was. In fact, it is normal to lose money occasionally when running any type of business. It's all part of the risk that every entrepreneur voluntarily takes when they venture out to work for themselves. Unfortunately, most young business owners don't expect to lose, so when they do, they aren't prepared mentally or financially. Many times if the loss is substantial, they eventually pack it in and give up. They go back to their safe zone, whatever that was to them. In most cases that safe zone is some form of employment, where they aren't risking their own money and usually where they aren't as passionate or as happy.

A lot of people like safe, and that's not necessarily a bad thing, so long as it doesn't keep you from doing the things you love or keep you from growing, but if you want to be an entrepreneur you have to be willing to let go of that safety net and take chances. It doesn't mean you become completely reckless and start making careless decisions without thinking things through, then cross your fingers and hope for the best. That is called gambling, and that is what casinos and lottery tickets are for.

There is a big difference between gambling and investing. When you are investing, you are doing lots of research before you plunge in financially, and you are making educated decisions based off of proven methods that actually work. You might lose, but you greatly increase your odds of winning because you are prepared and you have a plan. The more experience you gain in your field of investment, the greater your chances of winning and increasing your winnings are over time. That is not at all how it works at the casino or even in the stock market, especially when you let someone else invest your money for you. Gambling is when you put your money in, roll the dice, then hope for the best. Mostly when you gamble, you don't do any prior research on where you're sticking your money, and you are giving up control by allowing a machine, an unpredictable market, or someone else to dictate how to invest your money and what the outcome will be on your investment. I don't know about you, but I like to be in control of my own money and not leave it up to someone else or to fate. So now that you know the real difference between gambling and investing, how are you going to have the guts to take some chances by making tough but good financial decisions without being too careless with your funds and rolling the dice on financial decisions that are purely based on luck?

Personally, I have never felt that lucky when it comes to making uneducated guesses or letting someone else decide for me. I love the idea of being in control of my own life and being responsible for my own fate. I realize that there will always be things in life that we have little to no control over, but I believe in controlling what we can and adjusting the best we can when life throws unexpected darts in our direction. That is just part of life, and we can either let it defeat us by bringing us to the point of an unwillingness to take any chances at all or we can embrace the unpredictability of life by letting go of our fear of failing and go for our dreams. When you are getting ready to take that big financial chance on yourself or your business, just remember that failure is likely at some point, even if you think you've done all of the research you possibly can. But that's okay. Just make sure that when you do, fail small—especially when starting out—so it doesn't set you back too much.

You will learn more from those small failures than any school or training could ever teach you. I call this the school for the hard knocks, but it truly is the best education any aspiring entrepreneur can ever get: on the job learning. I can't put a price on the experiences I had as a young man of buying and selling cattle and how that has truly prepared me for what I am doing today in buying, selling, and renting out real estate.

I first learned how to make quick decisions on a small scale before I eventually was mentally and financially able to graduate from the cattle business to real estate, where the stakes are much higher because I am dealing with a lot more money. The important thing for me was that, like the house building analogy, I did not skip any steps. If I would have started buying and selling houses right out of high school, it would have been financial suicide because not only would I have had to borrow 100 percent of the necessary funds due to lack of finances, but I also would have lacked the investing experience and real estate knowledge needed to make such tough financial decisions. It would be like taking a third grader and dropping them off in college. Like I said, you can't put a price on real life experience, especially when it comes to smart investing and learning how to make good choices.

So what is being decisive all about? It's about your willingness to let go of your fears and make quick but educated decisions in life, either in investing your money or at any trivial crossroad that comes your way in your personal or professional life. At the start of this chapter I discussed how life is full of every day dilemmas and small decisions that force us to choose how we will respond to or approach situations as they come our way. We make decisions in our consciousness all of the time whether we want to or not. Even choosing not to act is a decision, and it is one that you and you alone can make.

Free will is a powerful gift that we have been given, so let's be wise with that power and not take it for granted. Use the power of free will to make your life the way you want it to go, not the way someone else or circumstance says it should to go. Decide today that you are going to start making choices that are going to empower you to pursue your own dreams and increase your chances of finding success, whether this be financially, socially, physically, or spiritually.

Anyone can train themselves to be decisive, but you can't procrastinate. You have to start learning to make difficult choices as they come; learn from your mistakes and live with the results. I promise you that as you do this and make it a part of your everyday decision making routine, you will be ahead of the curve and success will find you—so long as you don't give up on yourself or your dreams.

NOTES

CHAPTER 10

Stay Organized

I HAVE ALWAYS believed that organization is an essential part of running any business and keeping your life in order. It is what keeps us on schedule and on task to accomplish all that is needed in order to reach our day to day or long term goals. We live in a balanced universe that has laws and boundaries and runs in an orderly fashion. These laws are what keeps life going, and they protect the well-being of all who exist; they also keep all intelligent life in check. Yes, that includes each of us. Without boundaries and order there would be total chaos, and nothing would be sustainable or have real purpose.

Just take a look at the type of cooperation and discipline it takes in our own world to maintain a peaceful society, especially these days with there being so many of us. I can't imagine living in a world or a society without law and order. It would definitely not be a place where I would want to be or raise my family. We don't always like or agree with the laws we are each subjected to in this life, but the fact is, they are meant to keep us safe, and they help us live a happy and productive life. They are also meant to help us coexist peacefully with one another despite our many differences. I am amazed at what mankind has accomplished over the last 200 years or so as a global economy and at how far we have come as a people, in comparison to the thousands of years humans have roamed the earth. We have created a world where we can communicate with someone more than 10,000 miles away in the matter of seconds, and we can travel the same distance in just a few hours. We also live in a world where we can access an entire library full of information at the push of a button. We've adapted technology to do a job, which might have taken months manually, in a matter of hours or days. Technology has evolved the human race into very advanced societies and has made us much more economically efficient. In order to keep up with an advanced society such as ours it is vital that we not only educate ourselves on the world in which we live, but it is also essential that we learn to be organized in everything we do, so that we don't miss a beat in this rapid and ever changing economy.

Organization is what keeps us grounded and functioning when things get complicated, which they always do, and it is what helps us to keep focused on what we are trying to accomplish, so we stay on track. Believe me when you are working for yourself or are trying to run a successful business, especially these days, it is very important to stay on track and not lose focus on what you are trying to accomplish, be that the big picture or day-to-day operations. As an entrepreneur, you are responsible for all of the details that are required in order to run your business. As owner you are also responsible for the overall operations, which include personnel, services, company structure, and anything else important to the business. There are a lot of things to remember in running any business, so if you are not organized in how you keep track of it all, you will be unable to ensure things get done the right way. As a result, you will have a very hard time staying profitable, and you won't be in business for very long.

Before we get into why it's important be organized as an individual, I want to discuss what exactly it means to be organized. I have known many people who have a very difficult time with this particular character trait, and like most other traits I am discussing in this book, it is one that does not come natural for most. It is something you need to work on every day until it becomes habitual. Being organized includes: doing things to help keep you on task, so you don't forget what needs to be done; and preparing ahead of time, so that you have a well mapped out plan on how you are going to accomplish the goals you have set out for yourself or for your business. Some examples of organization are

1. labeling items that have specific purposes;
2. keeping specific notes for tasks you need to get done that day or week;
3. keeping a written schedule for important meetings or events you have committed yourself to;
4. making sure your work areas are clean, so you don't lose things; and
5. having a routine on how you prepare for events or simply how you work on your daily tasks.

These routines help keep you consistent in everything you do, and overtime, just like anything else, they become habits. Make sure you choose routines that are efficient and help you reach your goals the best way possible.

So let's talk about each of the examples I have just mentioned. Why is it important to get into the habit of labeling items that have a specific purpose? Well if you are running a store, shop, or a manufacturing facility of some sort, you are probably going to need some place to store your inventory, supplies, or tools needed to help your business function. If time is money, which in every business it clearly is, do you want to spend most of your time sorting through a mess because you didn't bother taking the time upfront to label what is what? This is especially important if you are hiring someone else to help you routinely fetch items out of your storage areas. Labeling items like inventory or supplies can also remind you on a daily basis of what you have on hand and how much of it you actually use, so you don't over order or forget to order something when you need it. Keeping important things labeled helps keep you organized and provides for you a well-oiled system that is there for you when you need it. Yes, it's a little more work up front and requires upkeep, but it is well worth it in the end. You can stay focused on the people and the important parts of running your business, rather than always scrambling for a lost item that you misplaced or buried because you didn't bother to label it in any way or form.

The second example I mentioned was taking notes on daily or weekly tasks. I can't over emphasize how important this organizational habit is. When I was first starting out in my real estate business, I would get overwhelmed very easily on all of the important little things I had to do and remember each day. I was new to remodeling houses, and I definitely underestimated how much there is to keep track of when you are renovating an entire house. There are so many details that you absolutely cannot overlook when you are taking a house from disheveled and unlivable to like new and profitable. It is a huge task and a very stressful step-by-step process, especially if you have very little or no construction background. So between overseeing the construction of our properties and dealing with all of the other details that were required to flip houses, I was having a very hard time remembering all of the day-to-day operations that I was in charge of. Even if I did remember all or most of the required tasks for that day or week, because I am a light sleeper and suffer from anxiety occasionally, I would find myself repetitiously over thinking each night about my to do list for the next day. I remember many sleepless nights running over everything I knew I had to do the following day, and it would drive me absolutely crazy to the point that when I woke up the next morning I would feel sick to my stomach due to stressing all night and a lack of sleep. I was trying to keep track of my to-do lists and all of my daily responsibilities in my head, and it was just too much for me. I soon came to the conclusion that I would need to start keeping a detailed personal list of all of the tasks I had to do and oversee that week, or even more specifically for that day for the business. Boy, did that make a huge difference for me! Not only did it make me more organized and efficient because now I was writing things down so I wouldn't forget, but I unloaded a lot of unnecessary nightly stress off of my shoulders. I no longer had to lie there in bed thinking and thinking about all of the things I needed to get done the next day or week. Now, I had it written down, so I could convince my brain to let it all go each evening and not to worry about it until it came time to actually work on my task list. I didn't have to worry about forgetting because now I had it in a physical notebook that I started keeping for my business. This may seem like a tiny thing for most people, but for me it was somewhat life changing. It made me more organized in my day-to-day responsibilities, and it reduced my stress at nights, giving me more positive energy in the mornings. So keep notes to help you keep track of your own daily or weekly tasks, and I think it will make a difference for you as well.

The third example that I want to talk about I believe goes hand in hand with keeping notes, and that is keeping a written down schedule of important meetings and events. I have always felt very strongly about being a man of my word when it comes to keeping the commitments I make with others, especially with those who are doing something that is benefiting my business. In my opinion, keeping commitments is how you establish yourself as someone who cares about what he or she is doing, and it establishes trust between you and those who work with you. Trust is very important when you are dealing with other people. So how does keeping a written schedule on a daily, weekly, or monthly calendar help you to keep your commitments to others and help keep you organized? Just like the note taking for your to-do list, keeping a physical schedule keeps you focused on what you should be doing from one moment to another and keeps you from forgetting about the commitments you have made with others, whether it be for your business, your work, or even your personal life. Keeping a schedule makes you much more efficient, and people will come to respect you because you are honoring them by doing what you say you will do and doing it when you say you are going to do it. I know this may seem like trivial common sense stuff, but I have always been amazed at how few people actually do what they say. They talk a good story then don't show up the next day. I am sure you know people who do this all of the time; if so, you know how frustrating it can be if you are the person who has been let down. So, be a man or a woman of your word and keep your commitments, it will make all of the difference in your relations with others you associate or work with. The safest way to make sure you are good at doing this is to keep an organized schedule with you wherever you go.

The fourth example I listed is to keep a clean work space. Now, for me, this has always come naturally because I am a little on the OCD side. I can't stand a messy room or work environment. I can't say the same for a lot of other people I have known throughout my life. I used to drive my wife crazy with my OCD cleaning habits, but I feel this has been more of a strong suit than a weakness. When it comes to working out of an office, which pretty much every business has, cleanliness definitely contributes to staying organized as an individual and business owner. I've been in offices, shops, and homes where there is stuff piled up all over the place to the point where you can't even see what color the desk or table is because it's covered in junk. (I usually consider things "junk" if they're piled up and not stacked nicely.) These messy work places make it very difficult to stay on task and even more difficult to find important documents, supplies, or tools. It also sends a very clear message to all those who enter that you don't care and that you are not an organized person. I remember a CPA we hired as a business that had a hard time staying on task and getting our taxes done in a timely manner, a direct result of the mess she had in her office. My business partners and I got to the point where we did not feel comfortable leaving important financial documents with her, as the messy stack of papers always found in her office meant our important documents could be lost. We decided to find a new CPA due in large part to the disorganization clearly displayed for all clients and potential clients to see. So, not only does having a messy work place affect you, but it can also affect those you work with to the point where they won't want to work with you any longer. On the other hand, I have been witness to many clean work spaces that have made a positive impression on how I felt about that particular business or person. For me, when the office I am working in is clean, papers are put away or stacked nicely, and stuff isn't randomly thrown all over the place, I feel so much more at peace and in control. I feel the same way about the houses we are working on; when the guys keep the construction project fairly clean while they are working, the remodel just seems to go a little smoother. Guys aren't feeling so scattered while on the job, and I along with them am able to see corrections that need to be made much easier than when tools and supplies are scattered all over the house. It has been proven that a clean space helps you better organize your thoughts and helps you think much more clearly. This goes with your personal residence as well. It is a great feeling coming home to a clean well-kept home after a long hard day at work. It is hard to relax in a messy home. Keeping your home or work place clean is truly another great way to stay organized in both your business and personal life.

The fifth and final example I mentioned as a way of being organized is learning to have a routine on how we go about preparing ourselves for and accomplishing our tasks we set out to do. What does it mean to have a routine? Well Dictionary.com defines the word routine as "a sequence of actions regularly followed; a fixed program." This basically means that you find something that works for your situation, you stick to it like clockwork until it becomes a habit or a part of your daily schedule. When I started writing notes for myself and doing other little things to help keep me on track, it wasn't always easy to remember to do these things every day, but as I started noticing positive results for myself and even for the business because of these new things I was implementing, I would make stronger efforts to turn these good habits into a part of my daily routine. Having a good routine, especially when you are working or doing something productive, is everything. It pretty much defines you in the workplace, and it can determine whether you end up successful or not. We all have some sort of routine, but not all routines lead to our success and contribute positively to our well-being. I am speaking of routines that keep your life in order and keep you doing positive and productive activities, which ultimately will lead to you accomplishing your goals in life. Remember, life is not just about the big crossroad moments, but rather all of the little day-to-day, minute-to-minute moments where you are regularly deciding on how you are going to live your life. So create for yourself positive routines that will help you be more organized in your life and help you to take control over how you want your future to go.

So, now that we have explored some great ways to be more organized in business and in your personal life, I want to address the question I asked earlier about why it's so important to be organized. Like I discussed at the beginning of this chapter, we all live in a universe and world that subjects us to laws, order, and boundaries. We can either choose to cooperate with these set laws, or we can fight them and suffer the consequences. I think most of us choose to try to abide by the rules of the world presented to us, which can vary a little from one society to another here in this life. But I think it is safe to say that most of us are law-abiding citizens to our respected communities, or at least we try to be.

Despite our attempts to create order in our lives through making an effort to adapt to the rules and boundaries we are presented with as members of society, it is not always so easy to create order within ourselves or implement successful organization skills in our own lives. With all of that being said, it is 100 percent possible to take control over your own life and still live within the rules of your society. Part of that control is learning to be disciplined in everything you do. In order to be disciplined, I believe you must first learn how to be organized, which entails a lot of the things I have discussed in this chapter.

I believe that we are here on Earth, not just to live a mortal life and learn how to get along with other people, but also to learn self-discipline—to learn how to take control over your own life and decide for yourself how it's going to go. You see being organized goes so much further than just being a good labeler, note taker, scheduler, cleaner, and routine maker. It's about taking control and being the master over your own little world, whatever you envision that to be. I see organization as you choosing to put your universe or life in order and not allowing outside influences to do that for you. Whenever I see someone who is unorganized, I feel as if they are casually living their life, not really caring all that much where the wind blows them. However, when we strive to organize our lives by taking control and doing all of the little things that push us closer to our goals, we are telling the universe that we care about what happens to us.

Believe me, when you send a message like that, it cannot be ignored and neither will you. So, take control of your own future and decide right now that you are going to be better organized as an entrepreneur and even more importantly as a person.

NOTES

CHAPTER 11

Develop People Skills

You have probably heard the phrase, "In business it's not what you know but who you know that counts." The truth is that both of these things are very important and vital to the success of any entrepreneur who is starting out. But this statement is meant to remind us just how important it is to have social contacts in the world of business and investing. Knowing the right people can have an enormous impact on your success and how far you can go with building your business.

For example, just take a look at some of today's popular business shows like "Shark Tank" and "The Profit." The auditioning entrepreneurs who make a great impression get the opportunity to team up with these famous self-made multimillionaire investors, and almost always, they do much better with these new partners than they would have on their own. Many of them become multimillionaires themselves because they partnered up with very experienced entrepreneurs, who not only have tons of resources from their own past successes, but also carry with them a winning reputation that can't be ignored by the public eye. These small or struggling businesses often go from being unknown and insignificant to suddenly becoming very well-known and ultra-successful seemingly overnight. This is because they now have that key golden contact, which instantly attracts more customers and better vendors and allows their business to be able explode in ways they never imagined or thought possible.

Why do I bring this all up you ask? Because I want you to see how important having the right contacts can be to any new or struggling business. A key contact whether that is a lender, partner, client, mentor, vendor, or even an employee can make all the difference on whether or not you succeed as a business or entrepreneur. That crucial person, whatever their role, can be your ticket to opening that door you've been trying to open for so long but couldn't figure out how to do so on your own.

Now, I'm not suggesting that all you need to do is find that golden contact and suddenly all of your problems will magically disappear and money will suddenly pour down from out of the sky. You still have to do and become all of those things that it takes to become a successful person, but having that key contact in your back pocket can definitely give you that extra

CHAPTER 11: Develop People Skills

something you need to give you an edge over your competition, whoever that may be.

Now what does all of this talk about having key contacts have to do with people skills? Well, it's quite simple. You cannot convince someone to join your business or investing adventures if you can't connect with them in some way or form, ultimately convincing them that you are the real deal and that your business has true potential. You basically have to sell yourself; this is what it all boils down to. If you can't sell yourself and persuade others that you have what it takes to succeed, then they will most likely find someone else who can. One thing I've learned about most people is that they are usually attracted to bright and shiny appearances, and they will flock to wherever they feel they can best benefit. So, if you have something great to offer and you can find an effective way to show the world what that is, you will more than likely attract many people to your cause, and in the process, you can find that key contact that will help take you and your business to the next level. But you have to be able to put yourself out there, and you have to have the ability to use your words and social skills to attract people. This is why I truly believe that you cannot succeed in business without obtaining some form of people skills.

They say that communication is one of the keys to building a strong marriage; well, the same goes for obtaining and keeping strong business relationships. Without good communication, especially these days, it is almost impossible to get things done and function as an organization. Having the ability to express yourself in the right way and to get your point across in a way that others can easily understand is crucial in the business world. You must be able to relay a message to your clients or provide instructions to your workers in a clear manner that both gets your point across while showing you respect and value them. Keep in mind, too, that communication is not just how you speak; it's also how you listen. There will be many times when you need to stop talking and listen to what someone else has to say. This is not always an easy thing to do, especially if you have a lot on your mind, but it will teach you to have patience and show them that you care about what they have to say. It's also very important to note that when you are in the middle of a conversation, you can't always express what's on your mind or correct someone every time they say something that conflicts with your own ideas and opinions. This means no interrupting the speaker and ensuring you are listening to what they are actually saying, not merely planning what you want to say next.

Though I discussed this in a previous paragraph, it is important to remember that good communication communicates respect to those involved. Always show respect to people you are talking to and working with because everyone regardless of their background has something positive that they can potentially contribute to society. This leads to another point, remember to always be flexible to new or different ideas because they might work out better than what you first thought up, or they could possibly lead to something even better than either one of you originally thought of. This doesn't always mean that another individual's ideas will work out for you or cause your business to exponentially grow, but none the less they probably know something that you don't, so it's important to acknowledge their strong suits and show them some form of respect. I promise that if you treat others the way you would want them to treat you, as the golden rule clearly states, the respect you show to them will come back to you tenfold; furthermore, other people will definitely take notice and will want to work with you. Everyone wants to be respected, and we all like to be acknowledged for what we do right.

As far back as I can remember, I have always enjoyed conversing with other individuals, though it did not come naturally for me. I always felt that I was going to say something that would make me sound awkward, and for some reason, I never felt all that comfortable socializing with kids my own age. I always preferred speaking with adults, and I never considered myself to be a social butterfly. But, like the old saying goes, "practice makes perfect."

I was fortunate enough to grow up in a religion that gave me the opportunity to give talks in front of audiences as a young man and teach lessons in class room settings. I was also fortunate enough to serve a full time mission as a 19-year-old in a foreign area. On a daily basis, I was required to go door-to-door sharing my personal beliefs with complete strangers. For many young missionaries, this is a very scary thing to do, but the more you do it the easier it gets until it becomes routine. Even though as a young boy I was always a little on the shy and quiet side, these social church experiences I had growing up helped mold me into the person I am today.

On my mission, I learned how to listen to people who had problems, then come up with encouraging words to say without offending them, all while still getting my point across. Serving in Houston, Texas, I ran into a lot of people of diverse backgrounds, so it was very important for me to listen to their points of view on life before putting in my two cents. Listening was never a strong suit for me. I can remember way back in early grade school, teachers giving me a hard time because I was a terrible listener or wasn't paying attention, which was probably because I wasn't most of the time. Over time, I came to realize that it was very important to pay attention to the people I was trying to teach and talk to because many of them did not grow up with the same beliefs I had. They did not share many of my beliefs, and I needed to understand them before I could explain my point of view. Plus, because Houston is such a diverse city and people are all so different to begin with, I learned that you can't talk to everyone the same way because we all have different personalities and backgrounds. In just a few short months, I felt I had gotten pretty good at talking to different types of people and listening to their life stories, as I would share with them the things that mattered most to me and brought me happiness. It was quite the hands on learning experience for me, and it gave me a lot of confidence when it came to conversing with strangers and getting along with people of all types. Getting so many opportunities to speak in front of other people as a boy and as a young man not only provided me with experience on how to vocally interact with other people, but it also gave me confidence. This confidence gave me the courage to speak to others on a regular basis in ways that would help me grow my business.

My mission experience really set the tone for me socially because I got the opportunity to do a lot of one-on-one interaction, which is extremely important when entering the world of business. When you are talking to someone who might be a potential employee, a client, or a business associate, it is essential that you establish yourself as confident yet easy to talk to. There is a fine balance there, and figuring that out is vital when it comes to building and keeping business relationships. You can normally tell right away when conversing with someone if they are confident or not. You can tell by their posture or if they can look you in the eyes when speaking. You can also tell by the tone of their voice and the way they speak to you.

These skills I learned as a very young adult and the social confidence I gained definitely paid off for me as I began my business pursuits. When I started out in real estate, I learned quickly that it truly is a people business more than it is a numbers game. I spent a lot of time punching numbers on a calculator and on paper before making my first official purchase, thinking it was truly all about analytics, but as I started into doing the real thing, I began to realize that there were many different types of people I would have to deal with just to flip one house or own a rental property.

First, you have to deal with realtors and possibly the sellers on the buying end, then your hard money lender. After that, you have your insurance agent and, of course, your contractor and subcontractors, whom you depend upon to fix up the place. This is just the beginning. The projects themselves require numerous interactions with city inspectors, home inspectors, property appraisers, listing agents, and the sellers or their representatives. Once the project is complete, you still have more interactions. With rental properties you have tenants, the traditional lender, banker, property manager or property a management company, and applicants. Then, to top it all off, at that the end of the year you have to work with your CPA to handle your income taxes.

I learned pretty fast just how important the social skills I had gained from my church experiences were going to be in handling all of these different types of people, who were all a necessary part of the business I was in.

In the beginning, I have to admit, it was pretty scary dealing with experienced contractors, subcontractors, and handymen that were all older than me and having to tell them what I needed done. Plus, I felt very inadequate because of not having any real construction experience myself. The buying part for me was a little easier because of my experience buying cattle, and the realtors were pretty easy to deal with for the most part. However, the construction was and still is to this day by far the hardest part for me. I was definitely way outside of my comfort zone interviewing contractors and trying to talk construction when I had very little clue what I was doing or what I was talking about. I remember at times pretending that I knew what I was talking about, so I didn't sound inexperienced. Obviously, I wanted the guys to have some respect for me, but then I was always getting stumped on using the proper construction terminology when talking to them. I was learning on the fly, but that was when my listening skills that I learned on my mission would come into play. I would pick up on how they described specific details of the job and all of the different names for different supplies or parts of the house. Overtime, I began to gradually learn more of the construction language and phrases commonly used in that world, at least enough to where it actually looked like I knew what I was doing and talking about. That was critical if I was to survive in that part of the business and do well at it, which I eventually did.

Experience makes a huge difference, but we all have to start somewhere. When it came to remodeling the houses I was buying, I truly had to learn on the fly, which honestly for me has always been the best way to learn. Nothing teaches like real life experience. But it all comes back to learning how to listen and how to properly speak to your audience in a way that they will respect you and be able to work with you.

First, you must figure out who your audience is, then figure out how you are going to talk to them and deal with them in a way that shows them you respect who they are and what they can bring to the table. However, don't come across as too accommodating or lacking in confidence, so they know you won't allow them to take advantage of you. That is where learning to speak with confidence really comes into play, and you get that through good old-fashioned experience and by paying attention to the people you are dealing with or talking to. As intimidating as contractors were to me at that time, inspectors were much scarier. Inspectors are very much like law enforcement. They are not there to promote themselves to you or help contribute to your business, but rather they are there to look for flaws and point out anything and everything you missed or did not do according to the current building code. No matter how good of a job you think you and your hired help did to remodel a house, inspectors always seem to find something, in many cases several things, wrong, and you normally have no choice but to make the correction if you want to sell the house and move on. Even more so than contractors, home inspectors really expect you to speak their language, and if you don't they will definitely hold that against you. One thing I have noticed about city or county inspectors is that they do like it when you ask them good questions and show them respect by politely accepting their advice or corrections. You also have to learn not to speak too much when they are walking the project with you, and they definitely expect you to know construction. I still to this day am somewhat terrified of any kind of inspector. They are by far my least favorite people in the real estate business, and they do not care how much money they're costing you. However, like many other jobs it is a part of the business I have no choice but to deal with. When it comes to all of the other people I have had to deal with in real estate, I have actually enjoyed conversing with them for the most part. At first, it was a little scary talking with hard money lenders and asking for loans, but I have always been pretty confident when it comes to dealing with the financial end of business, so it wasn't too bad.

Stemming from this, the second thing you need to do is to approach each negotiation or conversation with the knowledge that while you have your own agendas and goals to meet, the other person has their own point of view and their own agenda to accomplish as well. You have to figure out how to satisfy their needs without compromising what you are trying to accomplish, or they will not want to work with or do business with you. The same would go for any of the other people I had to deal with in order to make my business go.

Third, I always tried to treat everyone with respect, acknowledging their unique set of skills and how they were important to what I was trying to accomplish. Like I said earlier, everyone in this world has something to offer, you just have to figure out how you can best utilize them in a way that would benefit what you are trying to do, while always making sure that you have something to offer them in return that makes the relationship equal or fair for both sides. That is how a business relationship is supposed to work.

If you approach all of your relationships this way, people will want to work with you, and that is something you can't put a price on.

A final aspect of dealing with people who either work with you or for you is knowing how to encourage or correct them in a way that is effective yet does not offend them or make them feel defensive. The way I have tried to approach a situation where I walk into a project house and there are more negative things going on than positive is to first find something positive to say, making the guys or the contractor feel good about what they are trying to accomplish for you. Then, I gradually bring up things they need to work on or correct, but I continue to do it in a way that does not come across as though I am attacking them or insulting their work. For example, I could tell them something like, "I really like how the tile backsplash turned out in the kitchen, but I don't think we can leave those doors looking like that, what are your thoughts?" Or I may say, "I'm really impressed with your woodwork skills on that stairwell, but come take a look at the flooring over here in the corner. You see how there are large gaps? Buyers can be very picky about things like that, so we need to make sure we fix that and be a little more careful on things like that in the future, do you agree?" Rather than insult their work and focus only on their flaws, find something encouraging that you can say to them if you can and correct them in a way that doesn't make them feel like a failure or make you come across as a jerk who only sees what they do wrong. There are many ways you can make corrections without being critical or too negative, so practice them. It's important to build people up who are trying to contribute to the success of your business; not to tear them down. There will be times when you will have to be harsh to get your point across or even times when you have to part ways with someone, but you can still do so in a polite and respectful way without putting them down or raising your voice. As a part of this, it's always important to try to separate your personal feelings and emotions from your business. Be professional when you are dealing with people in the work place, and it will make your job a lot easier in the long run. An example of how you can let someone go without getting dramatic or hurting their feelings is to say something like "I appreciate your effort and everything you've done for me, but I really need someone who can keep up with the rest of the crew. I'm sorry but I'm going have to let you go." Or you could say "You're a great carpenter, but I know you are having a hard time getting along with the rest of the guys, so I think it's best if we just part ways." You see what I did once again in these two examples? I came out with a compliment first, so they let their defense guard down, then let them know what they did wrong and let them go in a way that didn't involve insulting them or attacking them personally. Sometimes it's difficult to know what to say when you're in the moment, but if you leave your emotions out of it and think before you speak, you will usually figure out the best way to get your point across to someone who has failed you in some way. With practice and experience anyone can improve in this area, until over time it becomes who you are and how you deal with every socially interactive situation.

We have been placed in a world full of people of all different types, backgrounds and personalities. You can't succeed in anything business or personal until you figure how to get along with other people and know how to interact with them. Whether it is a personal or a business relationship, always remember to show respect for the other side and find that balance between trying to help fulfill their needs and attempting to keep yourself on track to accomplish your own goals. You need to also remember to listen to what others have to say because two minds are always better than one, and you can't grow your business if you are trying to do it all yourself. You also can't overcome obstacles or learn anything new if you don't open your mind to new ideas that others may have. Take in what others have to say with a grain of salt because their way just might exceed yours or at least add to what you are currently doing. If you want that key person or contact that will make all of the difference in your business, learn how to sell yourself without compromising who you are deep down inside. Last of all be respectful in how you treat others and talk to them, because you want people to enjoy working with you. Positive reinforcement encourages others and usually brings out the best in them, which benefits you in the long run.

So start working on your own relationships right now and remember that your people skills will not only give you leverage, but they will give you a network of contributors that can truly take your business to the next level.

NOTES

CHAPTER 12

Aspire to Be a Good Leader

ANOTHER VERY IMPORTANT step that must be taken in order to become a successful entrepreneur is learning how to be a good leader. The ability to lead others in a way that inspires success and productivity is vital in the world of business. Most people are completely satisfied living their lives like everyone else, following the crowd and not taking the initiative to think for themselves. There are also a lot of people who are scared to death of being in the spotlight and would prefer to hide away in a safe corner where nobody can hear them or see what they are doing. If you want to be successful in the world of business, you cannot shy away from others, and you definitely have to learn to think for yourself.

This world is full of people who have what I call "the employee mentality." They wake up, go to work, do exactly as their told, then they go home where they try to forget about their work. The next day, they wake up only to do it all over again; it's a cycle. They get stuck in an endless rut of following somebody else's orders all of the time and doing the same thing every day, never aspiring to do anything different or become something greater. It's like being on a hamster wheel; they become so comfortable just running in a circle that the thought of getting off or running in a different direction terrifies them. Now, I am not saying that being a follower or an employee is a bad thing. Society needs people who are willing to work for others, and everyone has to learn to follow sometimes. But if you want to break away from the pack, become your own boss, and run your own business, it is very important that you learn how to become not just a leader, but an effective leader.

What do I mean by that? Well, a leader is someone who directs others and tells them what to do, but an effective or good leader directs by example and inspires others to do the same. They give direction, but they do it in a way that inspires others to do their best. They themselves are willing to make whatever sacrifices are needed in order to produce successful results.

As a business owner and an investor, I have had to learn for myself what it takes to be a good leader by treating the people who do work for me with respect and integrity. If I neglected to do this, I don't think anyone would want to work for me, and if nobody wants to work for me, my business would not be very successful. I would wear myself out by trying to do everything on my own. The ability to leverage yourself is the key to growing your business, and you can't do that if nobody is willing to work for you. As a business owner you have to depend on other people to help you out, but if you want them to stick around and do a good job, you have to learn how to treat them, and you have to be a good leader.

I have had many opportunities in my life where I was put in a leadership position of some sort, so when it came time for me to run my own business and hire other people to do work for me, it came somewhat natural. But like anything else it took practice and real life experience to hone these leadership skills.

You could say that my first leadership role started when I was a young boy. I was the oldest out of four children, and as the oldest sibling and only boy, I was expected not only to be a good example to my three younger sisters, but also to be somewhat of a protector for them. As oldest, I was always the first to do this or that, so I didn't really have that older sibling to look up to or learn from; I was it. I took my role very seriously because I did not want my younger sisters to see me as a disappointment, and I wanted to be a positive role model for them. I wanted to be a good mentor.

Another aspect of my life that provided new leadership opportunities was growing up in a church where the members even from a very young age are expected to participate and help the church function as a whole. I was provided many opportunities to teach lessons, give talks, and serve as a leader, which means I was given the chance to preside over a group and make important decisions for that group. Church callings and responsibilities always gave me a sense of purpose and responsibility. It gave me the opportunity to learn how to lead others and how to take stewardship over a position that had a part in helping to make the church function at least at a local level.

As an older brother in a religious home and a devout church-attending Christian I have always been expected to be a good example to those who were younger than me. As a teenager and young adult, I had quite a few people who looked up to me, and I did my best not to disappoint or let them down. I always saw myself as a leader because of how I grew up and due to the fact that I have always acted older than my age. For me, I guess you can say it felt somewhat natural, but I still needed these experiences as an older brother and as an active church participant to enhance my ability not to be merely a leader, but to be a good leader.

Not everyone has the natural ability to lead, but I believe anyone who truly wants to become such can do so with opportunity and lots of practice. I have learned over the years that being an effective leader is more than just directing others and making decisions for a group or organization; it is also about being someone who is willing to give up their own needs for the betterment of everyone around them. So, I guess you can say that in order to be a positive mentor to others and make a difference in their lives, you have to be selfless and learn to think outside of your own little world. You have to be willing to sacrifice your own comforts and immediate desires in order to achieve long term results and success. You also have to think about those who are working with you or for you and make sure their needs are being met or taken care of; you cannot think only of yourself. I call this a willingness to sacrifice for the good of the group and the betterment of others.

One thing I've learned about doing business with other people is that as the boss or owner you always have to see the point of view of those you hire and constantly be creating win-win situations with them. If you only see your own point of view, then creating and keeping a good working relationship with them will be very difficult because you won't be able to figure out what they want or expect out of working for you. You really do have to pay close attention to the people you choose to hire or work with because everyone is a little different, and you simply can't treat every personality the same.

Apart from all of this, I firmly believe that to be an effective and positive leader, especially in the world of business, you should also be a good follower. I think it's necessary to experience for yourself the position of the employee or student, as this might better help you understand their needs and where they are coming from. This is beneficial because when you are

CHAPTER 12: Aspire to Be a Good Leader

positioned as the boss or mentor you will have a well-rounded view of those who are placed under your stewardship. In other words, you have to learn how to follow and take direction from others before you can lead and give direction to people you hire or mentor. It's like the old saying goes, "The student has now become the teacher." You have to be willing to learn before you can be ready to teach. The same goes for the relationship between leaders and followers.

Like I said earlier, not everyone, in my opinion, is meant to be a leader in the business world, but I do believe anyone can learn how to lead in their personal lives. Being a good leader can easily be compared to being a good parent, teacher, mentor, or example to the people in your life, especially to those who are younger or less experienced than you. So while not everyone will get an opportunity to be the boss or to own a company, everyone has the opportunity to be a leader in other areas of their life. We just need to learn to step out of our comfort zone and take advantage of the leadership opportunities as they present themselves. These opportunities can be used as valuable experiences that will help us become our best selves.

Another important aspect of good leadership is to always stay humble and respect the people who are working for your cause. When I started out in real estate, I had to get my hands dirty more than I liked, and I performed these tasks with very little outside help. I couldn't really afford to hire many staff members, so even though I knew very little about construction, I did what I could and got the jobs done. As my business grew, I was able to hire out the things I didn't like to do as much, until eventually I didn't have to do very much of the construction work at all. I was able to delegate and chose only to do what I wanted. I recognized something as my work force grew: the guys really respected me when I would choose to jump in and get my hands dirty from time to time. A lot of real estate investors in my position would have chosen to completely remove themselves from the construction, especially if they don't enjoy that part of the business—as is definitely the case with me. However, the fact that I was choosing to be hands on really earned their respect and seemed to motivate them to give it their all when they were working on one of my jobs. Plus, I felt like I was leading by example by getting in the trenches with my guys now and then.

As a side note, working rather than supervising was also a form of therapy for me, having grown up on a ranch doing physical labor. There is a lot of stress that comes from buying and selling properties, so the physical work would actually help alleviate some of that burden I always seemed to carry. For example, financially, whenever we were way over budget on a remodel, which seemed to happen all the time, I could save in labor costs by working myself.

I realize now that it was very important for the guys I hired to see me being willing to get my hands dirty because it made me look more like a boss or owner that really cared about his business and valued their contributions by putting myself in their shoes. Another important part of my being hands on with my real estate investments is that, as a leader and owner, I'm better able to keep some control over all of the details that add up to whether or not we make a decent profit at the end of the year. I think it's important for every entrepreneur to stay involved in the day to day operations of their business—no matter how large or small their company is. That is how you stay in control of your business, and that is how you become a more effective boss. When I see a business owner that rarely involves themselves in the daily activity of their own company, it looks to me like they don't really care all that much, and I am sure that is exactly how it looks to the people who work for them as well. But if you are the type of leader who is willing to do anything to help your own cause and if you show up when you're supposed to, you will earn the respect of those who are helping you to either build or sustain your business. Of course, this principle, like many of the others we have discussed in previous chapters, applies to anyone who wants more out of their life and who wants to be the best version of who they already are.

So, are you going to settle for less by following the crowd and going through the motions of life, or are you going to step up and be a leader by taking control of your own destiny? Do you choose to be a leader who just bosses people around and doesn't respect what your employees bring to the table, or are you going to choose to be a powerful example to those who work for you by practicing what you preach? Remember, all of the truly greatest leaders in the history of our society had one very important thing in common: they lead by example and by serving others. They put those whom they led before their own selfish needs, and that truly is the greatest secret to being a good leader—the realization that to lead means to serve. So, hopefully this chapter helped you figure out what it means to truly be a good leader and has helped inspire you to become one yourself.

NOTES

CHAPTER 13

Become a Problem Solver

IF THERE IS one fact that I have learned over the years about life and business, it's that problems are inevitable—whether we create them through our poor choices or whether they come to us by no fault of our own. Either way you spin it, life is full of problems, and we can either choose to deal with them or try to ignore them. You can't always control what happens to you, but you can control how you respond. Do you give up or do you analyze the situation and find a solution to the problem? This is a concept that has gotten me through a lot of challenges and road blocks that have affected my business or personal life in one way or another.

Most people spend their whole lives trying their hardest to avoid as many problems as they possibly can, and often times they choose to take the path of least resistance when the choice is in front of them. Generally, I think that to some degree we all fall victim to this way of thinking, and it is a natural human response to try avoiding problems as they come our way. Sometimes doing this can protect you from getting hurt physically or emotionally, but many times avoiding challenges can prevent us from growing as a person, and we can miss out on learning opportunities or opportunities that can lead to something great. Nobody likes problems, but they are not only a part of life, they are also essential to our progression as human beings. I have always been a firm believer that we can't grow without adversity. Now this doesn't mean we should go out looking for problems, believe me they will come on their own, especially if you choose to live the life of an entrepreneur. However, it does mean we should be ready for them when they do come our way, so the trick is learning how to deal with them and solve them. That is where the real growth comes—not necessarily just taking a beating but actually figuring out the best way to resolve our issues and coming up with ways to fix them. Learning how to deal with our problems in a way that helps best benefit us in the long run and also allow us to continue down our path to a successful life. So, while it is important that we endure our challenges as they present themselves, rather than run from them, it is even more important that we take some form of positive action and learn how to solve our problems, and this is what this chapter is all about.

CHAPTER 13: Become a Problem Solver

I used to look back at my earlier years in grade school and think what a waste of time it was to memorize so many mathematical formulas that I clearly never have nor probably ever will use in my life, even as a professional real estate investor. I use math every day, but it is always basic math, and normally I use a calculator, which was many times not even allowed in early grade school. I can't recall ever once needing to use algebra, geometry, or calculus for any of my business or personal financial activity, and punching numbers is a huge part of what I do for a living. When it comes to analyzing deals, budgeting, and calculating profits, basic math usually does the trick. I was decent with math in elementary school, but once I got into high school, it got a lot harder for me and became very stressful, definitely one of my least favorite subjects. I can't count how many hours I would spend after school and on weekends trying to stay caught up on my math assignments and trying to memorize what I always felt were useless formulas for the next big algebra test. But now, looking back, I am starting to realize the importance of spending all of that time and effort on math back then. It was never really about memorizing formulas; it was about learning the process of solving problems until I got the correct answer or result. Yes, it is true that most people will probably never use complex math in their later years, unless they grow up to be an engineer or a rocket scientist, but we all have to learn the process of becoming problem solvers. This skill can translate into many aspects of our life: business, work, or even in our personal lives. That was the most valuable part of doing all of those algebra problems as a youth—the process of learning how to get from A to Z.

There is an old saying that goes, "Where there is a will, there is a way." What does this mean exactly? To me this means that if you keep trying, even after many failed attempts, eventually you will succeed and find the answer you were looking for. The key is to never stop trying until you figure it out. Some of the greatest inventions and business ideas in our country's history were a result of someone's determination to keep plugging away until they got their desired outcome or result.

Some of my favorite quotes about problem solving come from Thomas Edison, one of the greatest inventors of all time. One goes, "I have not failed. I found 10,000 ways that won't work." In other words, he is saying it might take many failed attempts before you finally get it right, but the process is important. You also need to remain positive in your failure and change your perspective on failure to see them as learning opportunities. Another of his sayings is, "Many of life's failures are people who realize how close they were to success when they gave up." To me this means that you should never give up and stop trying because eventually perseverance will find a solution to your problem. I love quotes like these because they remind me of how important it is to keep trying no matter how insignificant or trivial your efforts may seem at the time.

The fact is, everyone has the potential to succeed in one way or another, and we all have the ability to overcome any obstacle that stands in our way. Unfortunately, we are all on different playing fields when it comes to how determined we are to overcome and solve our problems. Many of us give up way too easily because persevering takes a lot of effort, and not everyone is willing to try as hard as the next person. Not everyone is willing to do whatever it takes to be successful and in order to do that you have to be willing to endure to the end. See how perseverance, discussed in a previous chapter, is a vital tool in a successful entrepreneur's toolbox?

When I started flipping houses, I quickly realized that if I was to survive and make it as a professional real estate investor, I would have to completely eliminate my old way of thinking where I gave up the minute things got difficult. My new thinking had to be, yes I know this is hard and things are not going according to plan, but I have to do my best to finish what I set out to do because if I don't my real estate career is more than likely over. I had to keep the vision of what I aspired to accomplish through flipping houses constantly in front of me, so that every time I got discouraged and wanted to give up I would remember my goals and keep pressing forward, even when the situation seemed hopeless. That was where being a problem-solver would really come into play and get me through one difficult obstacle after another.

When you are flipping a house, there are so many things that can go wrong during the process. For starters, you are buying a house that is not financeable, so it requires cash or a short term high interest loan. In my case, I am

CHAPTER 13: Become a Problem Solver

working with fixer-upper houses that many people have passed on; many people do not want to deal with the number of repairs needed. Once you find the house, you have to find guys you can trust to do the repair work for you, as every unforeseen problem imaginable will pop up during the renovation; you will most likely be over budget and past your timeline, then you have to hope that after all that there is room for profit when you go to sell. It's not only the construction and renovations that have problems to solve, there is also the selling process. Once you think you've got it sold through an accepted offer, you have to wait anywhere from 30–45 days during escrow to collect your funds. During that escrow period, anything from a bad home inspection to the buyers not qualifying for their loan to the buyers simply changing their minds can cancel your escrow and throw your house back on the market, costing you even more time and money. Not to mention the issues that may arise with the county and city building inspectors constantly giving you correction notices and additional work to do to your house during the remodel phase to bring it up to code.

I bring up all of these obstacles because they are all normal everyday problems that I have had to overcome during every house flip I have done up to this point in my real estate career, and I don't expect that to change anytime soon. In fact, because of California laws getting so strict on business owners such as myself and an unfriendly real estate investing market, I don't expect things to get any easier. But that just means I have to step up my own game and be willing to do whatever it takes to deal with whatever problems come my way in the future. On the flip side, I am now much more experienced, so I know how to handle these types of situations as they come.

Furthermore, I have a lot more financial resources to back me up, but it wasn't like that in the beginning. I was putting everything I had, plus other people's money on the line, and I had no rental properties to back me up. I had quit my night job, so I didn't have that as a backup either. I had a family to support, so I knew that failing was not an option. There were times when I had a house or even several houses all fall out of escrow at the same time, and I still had contractors to pay, business bills to account for, personal bills to pay, and of course no other income coming in. The only way I made it all work was to temporarily borrow more money, as needed, to stay afloat; I also had to live off credit until a house would finally sell. It was scary at times, but my skills with money and my determination to get through it all by solving one problem after another saw us through each rough period until eventually we were able to build up enough rental properties through the profits from the house flipping to keep us afloat when a house wouldn't close on time.

When tough times hit, and sometimes they come in waves, you may feel like you're having difficulty just staying above water. It is important to have your vision always in front of you to remind you what exactly it is that you're fighting for. Find your motivation, then just take each wave of challenges one bite at a time, so that you don't overwhelm yourself and bring yourself to the point of giving up. That is how I made it through each problem or obstacle that stood in the way of me trying to reach my business goals. There were many times I felt I was close to giving up, but I would hang in there and take small steps if I had to. No matter how small the tasks, I kept moving forward, because I refused to accept failure as an option.

Now, when it comes to specific problem solving strategies, it's important to always keep an open mind and be willing to accept the help or advice of those around you. Like the saying goes, "Two heads are better than one." I believe the more heads you have access to, the better off you are and the easier it will be to solve your problems.

Let me give you an example of this from my own business experience. I had a house that we were trying to fix up, and there was so much work involved that the county treated it as a new build, which meant we had strict codes to follow, like installing fire sprinklers and so forth. Plus, the contractor did a really bad job, leaving us with a whole list of code violations we had to fix. We could not seem to get enough water pressure from the well to pass our fire-sprinkler test. There was nothing but finger pointing going on by everyone who was on the job, but regardless of whose fault it was, I was stuck with all of the problems. The county put a red tag on the house, so we couldn't even move a tenant in there if we had decided to postpone selling the property. We had all of this money tied up into this huge project that was already over budget, and now we had to find someone to complete all of these corrections the county gave us and figure out how to pass our water pressure test. With the help of my wife, my dad (who is one of my business partners), some handymen from another job, and a plumber we knew, we were able to knock out that long corrections list, and after some trial and error, we finally came up with a booster pump system that helped us finally pass our fire sprinkler water pressure test. It was the most stressful flip I have ever done because it felt like it was never going to end. Luckily, we were able to break even at the end of the day. I learned a lot of lessons with this project, but the most valuable one was learning how to solve problems when I really wanted to give up. I was so angry with our contractor, the crew, and the building department that I had trouble sleeping at nights. But it wasn't until I decided to put my anger aside, make the phone calls I needed to make, and get to work on solving one problem at a time that I was able to overcome this huge obstacle of a flip house. The main reason I brought up this story is to point out that I could not have gotten through this one on my own. I was able to assemble a team of different skills and personalities to help me get through the project and solve each problem until everything eventually passed and we were able to sell the house and happily move on. I have had to get through dozens of similar projects that presented similar obstacles and problems, but that one always stood out the most to me.

Another one of the keys to being an affective problem solver is having the humility and people skills to bring in a team of support when needed and knowing how to best utilize their different skillsets. That is what makes a good leader like we discussed in the previous chapter, but that is also another way you become an affective problem solver. I constantly have to lean on the help, knowledge, and skill sets of others in order to get through each of the renovations and flips that I take on as a real estate investor. I rely on my business partners for support and advice, contractors and handymen for their construction expertise, lenders for when I'm low on funds, and realtors to help get me through escrow. We were not put in this world to face problems on our own, but I believe that we were put here to learn how to help one another out and utilize one another's talents and abilities.

With my lack of construction knowledge and skillset, I have had to rely heavily on the savvy advice of those I hired to do the work. I always made it a point to let everyone voice their opinions and ideas on how to solve problems at the job site. It was then my job as the leader, to make the final decision on how to proceed. However, I respect their knowledge and experience, because as a good problem-solver, it is important to utilize your resources, so, more often than not, I go with what the lead contractor on the job thinks is best. After all, what is the point of hiring experts if you don't take their advice? So I try to focus on what I do best when solving problems as they approach, then try to identify the talent needed to solve problems in the areas where I am lacking. People and businesses are usually more successful when they can work together as team.

A final thing needed in problem solving is the ability to improvise and think quickly on your feet. There have been many times during a remodel that I have had to figure out ways to make something work in order to save money. I learned very quickly that when you are restoring older homes and you have a limited budget to work with, you can't always afford to replace everything you want; sometimes you have to improvise and find a way to work with you've got.

In ending I want to emphasize the importance of not only keeping your mind open to the advice of those around you when dealing with your problems, but also learning to be more creative. Take the time to brainstorm before you tackle your challenges. You can do this by writing or typing a list of ideas and possibilities on different strategies you can use to overcome whatever it is that is standing in your way. Do some private research on the subject and be open to all point of views, however silly or improbable they may seem to you at the time. Sometimes one crazy idea can lead to another and another, until you finally discover something you hadn't thought of before. It can actually work out just the way you needed it to. So, brainstorm in whatever way works best for you, do some research, and be flexible with any ideas that pop up in front of you. Remember, trial and error is how some of the greatest discoveries were made, and it can also be how you figure out the best ways to overcome and solve your own problems.

So, what problems are standing in your way that might be keeping you from achieving your goals in life? More importantly, what are you going to do about it? Remember, we all have problems; the trick is learning how to solve them so they make us stronger, not weaker. You just have to choose to be proactive rather than reactive. In other words, don't let your problems define who you are but rather decide today who you are and how you choose to deal with them.

NOTES

CHAPTER 14

Learn How to Analyze

As a real estate investor, one of my most important jobs is to analyze each situation and potential deal as it comes my way, then make an informed business decision based off of my analysis. The dictionary defines analyzing as, "To discover or reveal something through detailed examination." To me this means to closely look into each opportunity or crossroads as it presents itself by doing due diligence and research prior to settling on a decision.

You might ask, what am I looking for exactly when analyzing? I have four things that I look for when preparing myself to make wise decisions that pertain to running or building my real estate business. The first thing that I look for are any potential money costing pitfalls or in other words financial consequences. Before moving forward with any business related decision, I want to make sure that the choice I am making isn't going to cost me or my business any additional or unnecessary amounts of money, so I ask myself if this is going to make me money or cause me to lose money in the long run. I make my best effort to calculate my estimated expenses ahead of time, so there are no huge surprises when bills come due. Second, I look for all of the potential positives that might come as a result of my choice and compare them to the negatives or costs. I ask myself both how I am going to benefit in the long run by doing this and how those around me are going to benefit. I sometimes even count up those potential benefits to see what kind of potential I am looking at, especially with regards to making a profit. I want to make sure that all of the good outweighs all of the bad if I choose to proceed; the reward needs to be worth the cost. Third, I look to see how much time and how many resources it will take to accomplish whatever is needed to make that decision pan out in the end. They say that time is the most valuable asset we have because it is limited; what we choose to do with our time can determine how successful we are in life. Are we going to be wasting our time or using it to be productive and be doing something meaningful? Furthermore, when it comes to resources, they are sometimes limited as well, especially if you are just starting out. This means it is important to be wise with what you have available to you. Using too many resources or misusing what you have can lead to your business not having what it needs when it needs it. Keep in mind, too, a resource can even be a person with a specific skillset or an organization that can service your needs in one way or another; a tool or a product of some sort; or anything that leverages your ability to do something. The final thing I look for is whether or not my decision is going to have any additional negative consequences that may affect the relationships I have with others or deter someone of importance from wanting to work me or help me out. In my line of work, I am really dependent upon others to do for my business what I am not able to accomplish by myself, so it is critical that I keep my business relationships on good terms at all times. I have to be sure that whatever I decide is going to help me to maintain those relationships and not hurt them. Many people seem to get this false idea that many of their decisions don't affect others, but the truth is that most decisions, especially when it comes to business, affect more people than you probably realize. I call this the domino or ripple effect, so I always try to make sure that I am considering those who are current or potential future contributors to my business before moving forward with a decision.

Now that we've discussed a few ways on how to analyze a situation or a potential deal, let's talk about why it's so important to take the time to do these four steps I laid out. When it comes to investing your time and money into something, you have to realize that there will always be a risk of some sort. It could be the risk that you might lose money or break even, or it could be the risk that whatever you choose might have future personal or social consequences. Risk is just a natural part of life. We make decisions based on what we think is right or best for us, then we have to live with the results or consequences. Either way you are always risking something when you make a decision. The way you minimize that risk is by taking the time to analyze each scenario as it presents itself to you, and this is a process that should not be taken lightly if you want to have successful outcomes and ultimately be a successful individual or entrepreneur.

I have laid out an effective process that I use when making real estate investing decisions, but you will have to figure out a process that works for you and your situation or your business. Regardless of what it is, it is very important that you have a process. If you want to be a good decision-maker you have to be able to analyze your situation in a way that prepares you with all of the knowledge and insight needed to make the best decision possible. Another important thing I would like to add is that when you are going through the process of analyzing, don't get too caught up in seeing only the short term benefits or pitfalls to your decision. Try to open your eyes just a little bit wider and look for the long term benefits and pitfalls as well. Short term and long term both affect you and your business, so ignoring one can have disastrous consequences. Learning to have this mindset is truly what separates those who are successful in business for a few years versus those who set themselves and their business up to have success for a lifetime, or even for generations.

So if you are the type of person who is just thinking about getting by today and not considering tomorrow, I want you to start reprogramming your brain to think more long term. Start imagining what you hope your life or business will look like ten or twenty years from now, then make a plan on how you are going to get there. Make sure it is a realistic plan. As you begin your journey and start running into cross roads as they present themselves, step back, remember your vision for your future, and then make decisions that will best support your vision. Don't allow yourself to get distracted by shiny objects and temporary successes that might deter you from doing what is best in the long run. Be willing to sacrifice short term success for success that will last a lifetime. This concept applies to everything in life, and it has been one of the main reasons I have been able to build a successful business from the ground up.

This all goes back to learning and taking the time to properly analyze your decisions before you make them; in other words, think before you act. There have been many times when I have had to decide on whether or not to purchase a particular investment property, and I have then had to live with the results. You better believe that every time I was getting ready to spend tens of thousands of dollars on a distressed property, I took the time to make sure it was the right business decision that was going to be in line with my long term goals as a successful real estate investor. Does that mean that all of my purchases turned out to be successful? The answer to that is no. But my analysis most certainly minimized the risk I was taking by buying properties that had tons of issues and that other investors would pass on because of the amount of repair work needed.

As an investor you are always taking a chance that you might lose or break even, but you minimize that risk by taking the time to analyze the entire deal and by doing your research beforehand. In real estate, they call this "doing your due diligence." So what I do first is look at the house size, bedroom and bathroom count, location, and lot size, then I compare those to other similar houses nearby in order to see what they sold for in their fixed up condition. I physically go through the property very carefully, sometimes with my contractor, and look for all of the defects that will need to be repaired to make it look good again. These required repairs are added up in order to begin my project estimate. I always try to throw in extra for additional unforeseen repairs, as every project will have these. After that, I add up my holding costs, which include interest on my hard money loan, property taxes, insurance, utilities, and required inspections. At this point, I will look up the property in county or city records to see what permits were pulled, see if it's in a flood zone or not, check on well and septic, and sometimes even double check the zoning. Then if that all checks out, I will sometimes have specific inspections done to make sure my numbers are where they should be on my remodeling budget and ensure that I'm not missing anything. I acquire the funds needed to close on the property and proceed with all the renovations that are needed. Once I do all of that, I double check with my business partners to make sure we are on the same page with the purchase and renovation plans. When everything checks out and meets my criteria for selling or renting the property for a profit, I finally proceed with the process of purchasing the property and hope that I did enough due diligence to make sure that the decision I made was the right one.

Like I said, even after doing all of that research, there is still no guarantee that my outcome will be what I thought or hoped it would be; there is still the risk of losing or breaking even on my investment. But by taking the time to analyze the entire deal and doing my due diligence, I am minimizing my risk dramatically and giving myself the best chance possible to succeed. Looking back at all of the flips I've been a part of and all of the rental properties I've purchased, I can say from personal experience that the process of making calculated risks through properly analyzing each deal works, and I have about a 90 percent success rate. Out of approximately

70 investment properties that I have been a part of purchasing in the last nine years, only six or seven of these turned out to be bad investments, and I only actually lost money on two. Those are some pretty good odds if you ask me. Call it good luck if you want, but I truly believe that it was my good decision making process that helped me achieve such great odds.

These were all risky decisions, but they were calculated risks, which is not at all like putting your money in the stock market or going to the casino. There you have little to no control over what happens to your money once you hand it over; at least with investing in real estate or your own business you have some control. Of course, there will always be those unforeseen pitfalls that come with any investment in life, but if you do your part and educate yourself beforehand, you increase your odds greatly of hitting the jackpot and coming out successful on the other end. Once you find a recipe for success, you will find that it becomes a little easier to duplicate over time.

Now, there have been many instances when I did not have several days to make a decision on whether or not to buy a specific property. I have made about a twenty purchases as a part of online auctions and courthouse auctions. With online auctions you do get an escrow period, but you are making a decision on the fly on what you're willing to spend on a property, while bidding against other investors. So you have to already have in mind how high you're able to go in order to meet your criteria as an investor; you can't get caught up in what I call auction fever. I had a number in mind, and it was important that I stuck to that no matter what the other bidders online were doing. Now when it comes to the live auctions, you don't have the luxury of an escrow period where you have ample time to investigate the property before committing to purchasing it. Plus, you have to show up with a cashier's check for the full purchase price. You need to do all of your due diligence before auction day and stick to your predetermined number just in case you missed something. I always made sure that I came in a little lower than the highest price I was willing to spend on each property. This is because they were much riskier investments, so I want to make sure I was covered. Luckily, I've made really good profits buying this way, and my best deal to date came from showing up at a live auction and bidding on a property I didn't think I had a chance at winning. My ability to make this good investing decision on the fly came from the experience I had acquired from other purchases, which had allowed me to learn how to properly analyze an investment property for purchase. Over time, I have become confident enough to make these decisions a little quicker, as the occasion sometimes requires.

Like I mentioned before, all it takes is common sense and good usage of basic math to make an intelligent, calculated decision on whether an investment is a good one or not. It's so simple that a third grader could do it, but for some reason when it's money on the line, most people freak out, and their common sense goes out the door. For house flipping the formula for your money is sales price minus purchase price plus all expenses to equal profit. It's that simple, yet so few are able to do it successfully. The trick is learning how to analyze your numbers properly so your expenses plus purchase price come in lower than your expected sales price, but you have to do the ground work first to make sure you are not guessing. Your decisions should be based on facts. This formula pretty much works for all business decisions and can be duplicated over and over again once mastered.

I hope this chapter has been beneficial to your quest to becoming not just a decision maker, but a wise decision maker. The ability to analyze is an ability that anyone can obtain, and it can bring you a lot of financial or personal success if put to use in the right way.

CHAPTER 15

Develop the Ability to Negotiate

I believe that everyone in this world is entitled to their own ideas, opinions, and expectations of what or how things should be in their lives. This is a God-given right that we have each been given in order to allow us to create a satisfying life for ourselves. But it's important to remember that we all share this world. As members of a very populated planet, we are expected to use our free will of opinion in order to help one another create a society where we all have the opportunity to benefit. Since we are each unique in character, background, and personality, we are going to have differences in opinion when it comes to what should be or how things should be done. When it comes to doing business with other people, it is always important that you figure out how to find a fair middle ground that achieves what you are after yet satisfies the needs of those you work with as well. I call this negotiation, and it is something we all do on a daily basis whether we realize it or not.

Negotiating is a social interactive process where two parties with different points of view strive to come to a mutual agreement that satisfies both sides. In other words, it is a way to compromise and bring two different sides and opinions together in harmony, so the needs or wants of each person is being met in a way that works for them. But notice how I used the word compromise. What exactly does this mean? Let me show you some examples.

Take a look at your average married couple; you have two distinct people of perhaps differing backgrounds and potentially very different ways of thinking suddenly deciding to take their two worlds and combine them into one. The husband may be used to doing things one way, where the wife may be more comfortable doing that same thing a different way, but only one way is necessary or required to achieve the desired result. Perhaps the husband wants to live in the country, have a small house, and buy extra land to raise animals; however, the wife may prefer to live in the city and have a bigger house with only a small back yard to take care of. Another example could be that the husband prefers relaxing at home and watching TV after a hard day's work, whereas the wife would rather go out dancing or go to the movies after her day is through. Of course, since I mentioned TV and movies, the husband might want to watch sports or a violent action movie, but the wife may prefer reality shows or a romantic chick flick. Lastly, you have the famous battle over the toilet seat. One is used to leaving it up, but the other is used to having it down. Let's be real though, most guys lose this particular battle. I can go on and on with many of the differences that come with sharing your life with another person and living under the same roof as them, but the point I am making with all of this is that in every marriage or serious relationship there has to be compromise. Compromising means being willing to change or adjust your original way of thinking or doing things in order to accommodate someone else that might see or do things differently from you.

You may ask how does this tie into the ability to negotiate? Well, when you are trying to settle up on a decision or find common ground with someone who has totally different views or different needs than your own, the only way both sides can come to terms is if one or both are willing to compromise. Someone has to be willing to step off of their own pedestal of what they feel is best or fair, in order to make the other side feel like they are getting a good deal as well. I believe that in fair negotiations it is vital that both sides be willing to make compromises or at least be flexible enough to make some changes or adjustments in order to come to a mutual agreement of some sort. I want you to stop for a moment and think about all of the times you have negotiated with people in your life; think about the times when it worked out well for both sides versus the times it did not. It could be anything from negotiating with your child about how much of an allowance they should get for accomplishing all of their chores on time to negotiating with your boss or business partner on how much you should be compensated for your contributions. What did you or they do right that made the negotiations go smoothly and work out great for both sides? Or what did you or they do wrong that made things feel very uncomfortable and caused both sides to be unhappy with the outcome? Figure out all of things that worked most effectively and see if you can duplicate them for future negotiations, trying to build upon them the best you can.

As far as what you did that did not seem to work, be open to considering different ways of communicating your point of views for next time and be willing to change your strategy. The difficult thing with all of this, though, is that everyone is different, so what works for one person may not work for someone else. Furthermore, what worked or did not work in one instance may or may not work in a different situation. So you really have to pay close attention to who you're dealing with and what the circumstance is in order to figure out what negotiation strategy will work best. Like the saying goes, "Sometimes you just have to play it by ear." Anyone can become an expert in this area, like anything else it just takes experience and lots of practice.

Another important aspect to being a good negotiator is knowing the person whom you are negotiating with. What do I mean by this? Well, find out what is important to them and figure out what it is that they are hoping to get out of their business or personal relationship with you. Are they looking for a short term solution, or are they seeking something more long term? Are they in it just for the money, or does it go much deeper than that? Maybe, they just want respect and to feel like they are being heard out or understood. Or maybe they do not care about what others think, and they just want to get as much as they can out of the situation. Whatever it may be that is truly driving a person, it is essential that you find out as much as you can about them, so you know exactly what they want or are expecting from their relationship with you. In other words, you have to know what their motives are. Next, get to know them better on a personal level. Find out what they like or dislike. Are they interested in the outdoors, or are they more of an indoor kind of person? Do they like spending their time socializing with others, or do they prefer spending it alone? Also, find out how they think or what their belief system is. Do they wear their emotions on their sleeve, or do they keep it all inside? Is family or religion a high priority to them, or are they more into politics and entertainment? Do they have a sense of humor, or do they take things very seriously? These are the types of things you need to find out and know ahead of time if you really want to connect with someone and know how to best communicate with them. This is something I feel is crucial when negotiating.

Another important thing is to know how to read the situation and understand who actually has the upper hand. Once you know who you're dealing with and what they want or expect from you, it's important to determine who needs this the most and who suffers the greater loss if things don't work out. If it's them and they know that you know this, then you definitely have the upper hand, and they will be willing to lean your way a little or even a lot in order to work something out. The person who looks the most desperate usually loses when it comes to getting their way. On the other hand, if you appear to look more desperate then they have the advantage because they see that you need this more than they do. This means they may not be willing to budge or lean your way at all. Therefore, I feel that it is important not look desperate when in the middle of negotiations; the moment you do, most likely, the other side will take advantage and choose to stand their ground a little firmer on what they are hoping to get out of the deal. They might even decide to ask for more if they feel they can get it out of you.

The game of poker is probably the best analogy I can think of when it comes to negotiating, especially in business. It's crucial that your opponent not know what type of hand you are holding, or they will respond in a way that best benefits them. If you have a good hand, do your best to keep that to yourself, so that your opponent thinks they have a good chance of beating you and decides to bet more because they believe they have the better hand. If you have a bad hand, then you do not want the other side to know because they will use that information to their advantage and get as much as they can out of you, knowing now that they can beat you. You need to keep them guessing, and your facial expression or lack thereof can give you away, giving them the advantage. This is only the case if they don't give themselves away. I hate comparing real life business or even important personal negotiations to a gambling card game, but that is exactly how it works in the real world. The person who speaks first or shows his cards too soon is usually the one who loses and ends up not getting their way, sometimes losing out on making any sort of deal with the other side. You have to learn how to show your "poker face" as they call it.

Being a real estate investor, negotiating has probably been one of the most important traits for me to get good at because it is something I have to do all of the time, especially when it comes to buying or selling property. Good negotiations are how I have come to make some of my best deals—

whether it is on the selling or buying end of the business. When I see a property that I like and it looks like it has great potential, I approach it with my best poker face possible. I don't let the seller or even the agent involved know that I am excited about buying it or making a profit off of the purchase. Instead, I start looking for flaws in the property and start mentioning all of the work and money that I am going to have to put out in order to make it work for me. I don't want them to think I'm desperate, and I want them to believe that I have plenty of other options if this one doesn't work out—even when I don't. I want them to know during the negotiation phase that I am willing to walk away if they don't agree to the price I want to pay. I also try to find out why they are selling, so I see what the motivation is to sell at a discount. If I can get that answer, then I'm getting exactly what I am looking for. I also try to get a feel for how low they will go, so I can get the best deal possible. It also helps my cause if there is very little interest from other investors, so my offer will be the only offer they are getting, making it more appealing. If that's the case, then I would have a huge upper hand over the seller, but if not then the advantage would swing their way.

If I make my offer and they don't accept, the real negotiating process begins. It's time to see who is more desperate, the seller or the buyer. They will usually counter my original offer, which is typically on the low side if there is no competition. I then counter back, always keeping in mind where I need to end up or what my limit is. It is important when negotiating to not get caught up in the hype or in your emotions. Always to stick to your guns by remembering what your goal is. Don't let the other side cause you to forget what you need and what your limitations are.

Sometimes during a back and forth with either the seller or my potential buyer, I will be patient and not respond immediately, even if I already know what my number or response is going to be. This can make them think I am not desperate and that I truly am willing to walk away from the deal. I want them to sweat a little, but like I said earlier every deal and every person is different, so that does not always work to my advantage. Sometimes I feel it is important to respond quicker or come back with a better price, so I don't offend the other party and potentially lose out on a great deal. Again, I have to know who I am dealing with, so I make the right moves and perform the negotiation in the right way.

Once I am in negotiations with a buyer or a seller I usually find a way to make sure we come to terms because I don't want my business to be stuck in neutral over pride or greed. I want to be able to make a deal, so I can move on to the next project and keep things moving forward. A lot of people lose sight of the big picture and forget about what they're really trying to accomplish in the long run because they are too stubborn to compromise and make a deal. They either get offended, or they get too greedy. Usually when this happens, those people never end up getting anywhere because they are too caught up over one negotiation that didn't go their way.

Don't let this happen to you. Don't let others take advantage but learn to compromise when you need to. Don't forget to be flexible if the other side isn't doing what you thought they would. Life is too short to get hung up over one bad deal, so move on. Believe me, there are plenty more potential good deals out there to be had.

Experience really is the key when it comes to being a good negotiator. The more experience you get and the more people you work with the better you will be at learning how to read others and knowing how to get what you want out of life. I am not suggesting that you use your expertise to take advantage of other people, especially those who are weaker or less experienced than you. This interferes with your overall integrity, which I feel is very important to have if you want to live a happy life and be loved or appreciated by others.

Like everything else there has to be a balance. It's important to do what's best for your life, but it's also important that you help others to do the same and be considerate of their lives as well. I am simply saying that if you want to succeed in a competitive world you have to learn how to deal with other people and learn how to be a good negotiator. This is a skill that you will use not only in doing business but in every important aspect of your life.

So, the next time you are negotiating with someone, remember these important tips: know who they are, figure out what they want, understand how to read the situation, show your poker face, and always keep in mind what it is that you want or need. If you can follow these steps every time you are trying to make a deal with someone, I promise that you will become more powerful than you realize, and you will become an expert negotiator. Once that happens, anything is possible!

NOTES

CHAPTER 16

Figure Out How to Leverage Yourself

As a kid, one of my proudest moments and academic accomplishments came in the middle of my eighth grade year. I was attending a very small country school, which I had been going to from the time I was in the third grade. Every year we would do a science fair with two other similar, small schools, and we were given the freedom to select a scientific subject of our choice then come up with a hands-on experiment, a report, and a large display illustrating all aspects of our chosen subject. I always looked forward to these science projects because it gave me the opportunity to freely express my field of interest, and it gave me the chance do something on my terms. That particular year, I chose to do my project on "The Power of Levers." I wanted to do something that was very applicable to the world in which we live and also something that was fairly easy to understand yet remarkable at the same time. So I built a long wooden lever with a certain amount of number labeled notches to illustrate how every time I would move my lever one way or another notch by notch it would determine how easy or how difficult it was to lift a certain amount of weight. For example, if I moved it close to my base, or the fulcrum, giving me a shorter lever, it was difficult to lift something heavy, but if I moved it in the other direction, giving myself a longer lever, then it became much easier to lift that same amount of weight. I was displaying the concept of how through the usage of levers we can lift more weight than if we tried to lift it on our own and how the longer the lever we have the more weight we can lift. There is a quote given by the famous Greek mathematician and astronomer Archimedes that I remember stating in my report. He said, "Give me a lever long enough and a fulcrum on which to place it, and I shall move the world." After finishing putting together our science projects, we got together with the other schools at a science fair and competed by setting out our displays and presenting our projects to three different judges. Apparently, I made quite the impression with my simple yet practical project on the power of levers because I won first place out of thirty one seventh and eighth graders. As an adolescent this was probably the proudest moment I can recall because it was the first and only time I had ever won a first place trophy in anything. Little did I know then, but that simple elementary school project would serve as a platform and a powerful lesson for me later on in life.

CHAPTER 16: Figure Out How to Leverage Yourself

What I am referring to now is a different type of leverage, but it uses the same concept: we have the ability to do more with less, but this is something we must figure out how to do effectively in order to make it work in our own life. It's a pretty cool comparison if you stop and think about it. Just look at how levers give us an advantage by making us seem stronger than we really are by giving us the ability to lift an impossibly heavy object off of the ground when used correctly. Just like in my science project display, the longer the lever the more power to lift. The same goes with running a business. You can choose to do it all on your own with limited resources and using just your own hard earned cash to operate, or you can choose to leverage yourself through hiring other skilled people to help you get much more done and use the banks or other investor's resources to provide you with additional capital to grow your business even faster.

I have seen many mom and pop investors or business owners who bust their butts every day, trying to do everything on their own. Many of them either just don't trust anyone else with their business or don't feel they can do as good of a job; when it comes to borrowing money, they are scared to death because they were taught from a young age that debt is bad. So they run around trying to do it all on their own, and in many cases they run themselves into the ground because without them physically being there doing all of the necessary day to day to operations, their business ceases to exist, and they stop making money. They can't afford to get sick, injured, or take a vacation. Their business is 100 percent dependent upon them being physically present and active to make it run. I don't know about you, but that to me seems like insanity. If you are going to work like that, you might as well work for the government or a huge company with benefits and a pension plan. At least then at the end of the day when you are too tired, too sick, or even too old to keep up that demanding work pace, you at least have some sort of residual income or retirement waiting in the works. When you work for yourself, you have none of that. It is up to you to provide your own retirement plan. If you don't, you will most likely be forced to either live out your days living way below your current financial life style or you will have to work until you die. I don't know about you but neither one of those options sound very appealing to me.

You see, leverage gives you the ability to avoid all of this by allowing you to live off of a system that you have created or built up. When you leverage, you can step out of your business, as needed, and serve as a manager and overseer, rather than serving multiple roles and attempting to do everything yourself. I call this part of business working smarter, not harder. Now don't get me wrong, if you remember my earlier chapter on developing good work ethics, it's important to learn how to work hard, and I very much believe in the concept of earning what you get. However, if you never learn how to leverage yourself, you will burn out eventually, and it will be difficult to grow your company.

There is a story that I love that really illustrates this concept best. It comes from one of my favorite authors, Robert Kiyosaki, who is most famous for his book called *Rich Dad, Poor Dad*. There was an Indian tribe that was in desperate need for a water supply to keep the people alive, and they were looking to hire one of their own to help solve this dilemma. They needed someone to find a way to provide water for their village. There were two volunteers. One was a large and strong man, who decided he would run down to the nearest lake, fill his buckets to the top, then rush back to the village, repeating this process every day and making as many trips as he possibly could. By doing this, he could get water to the village immediately. But they found that after many trips even this very strong tribe member would tire out and start to slow down over time. The other volunteer was a smaller man not nearly as strong as the first, but he was quite intelligent and creative. This man knew he couldn't be very effective carrying buckets of water every day, so he decided it would best to come up with a system that would supply water without having to run back and forth like his competition was doing. He took the time to recruit some of the other tribal members to help him build a pipeline that would start at the nearest lake and end at the village. He wasn't immediately able to bring water to his village, as the first volunteer had, but once the project was completed, he was able to sit back just keeping an eye on his pipeline, while water was being transferred automatically every day from the lake to the village. He found a way to solve his village's problem without running himself into the ground and by using his intelligence and creativity to create a system that did the hard work for him and was much more effective. He was doing a lot less work than his competition, yet he was providing his village ten times the water supply. He did not let his pride or his ego get in the way of trying to figure out the best way to solve a problem and getting an important job done for his people. So, you can probably guess who the tribe hired for the job, or at least who they gave the most credit to for their survival. The difference in the story is that one man was basically living in the moment and providing water for his people on a day by day system, while the other was living for the long run setting himself and his village up for a lifetime supply of water.

So, what are you going to do? Are you going spend your time carrying around buckets, providing just what you need to survive in the moment, or are you going to take the time to use your creativity and the resources God has given you by building pipelines that will provide you with a lifetime of success? This is a question that you and only you can answer, but it is one that you need to ask, especially if you want to be an entrepreneur.

I love what Robert Kiyosaki says after telling this story. He says that when doing business, he always asks himself, *Am I carrying buckets or am I building pipelines?* I try to ask myself the same type of question when I am trying to get something done within my own real estate investing business. Am I doing things the hard way by trying to do it all by myself and not using effective methods, or am I going to be smart by recruiting the proper help I need to get more done and utilize all of the resources that are at my disposal? I honestly believe that God has given each and every one of us all of the resources we need in this life to succeed, but it is truly up to us to find them and figure out how to best use them.

This is especially true for those of us born in the United States of America, at a time where there is so much information available, technology, finance options, and the freedom to do or be whatever you want. We are truly blessed to live in these modern day conditions where we are given all of the resources needed to succeed if we just take the time to learn how to properly use them to our advantage.

The concept of using leverage in business is broken down into two basic types of resources. The first is other people. For me growing up on a small ranch I wasn't really taught the concept of using other people to build a successful business. I was operating my buying and selling cattle business on a very small scale, so I pretty much learned to do almost everything myself. If I decided not to work that day, nothing would get done, and my chores would be there waiting for me the next day. I had to work hard every day that I possibly could if I wanted positive results for my small business. I was learning to have a great work ethic, but I was not learning the power of leverage. I relied on me and me alone. I was putting myself in a position where I would always have to rely on my ability to go out and do all of the physical labors myself in order to provide a living, which was fine while young and healthy, but I knew I wouldn't stay that way forever. Deep down inside, I knew that I would eventually have to find a better way to set myself up when it came time to retire and when I was unable to do all of the hard work that was required as a cattle rancher. It didn't take me long to realize this, and I knew I needed to make a change if I wanted to provide a good living for me and my family for years to come.

When I started out in real estate, I learned very quickly that I would have to drop the idea of me trying to do everything myself, even though that is how I operated as a cattle rancher. I was now in a whole new world that I knew very little about, and I could definitely not go at it alone. I needed all of the help I could get, so I started to change my old way of thinking by adopting a new and smarter way. I focused a lot of my efforts on seeking out other experts in the field of real estate and construction and seeing how I could pull them in to effectively use them to help me to succeed at what I was trying to accomplish as an entrepreneur. In my case, it was learning how to buy, fix up, and sell or rent a property for a profit. There was no way I was going to be able to accomplish such a daunting task on my own, so like the individual who was looking to more effectively provide water to his village by building a pipeline, I started to work on building my own pipeline by recruiting others to my cause, as I was able to. I assembled a real estate team by forming business partners, hiring contractors, and using other real estate experts to get through my first flip. Then, each time I moved on to the next project I would have even more means than I did previously to leverage myself through hiring additional people to help build up my little real estate empire one transaction at a time. It pretty much snowballed from there as I learned to reinvest most of what I made into the next purchase. That is how I was able to actually grow my business, but it started with learning to accept the fact that I could no longer do it all by myself. I had to have the humility to understand that I would need lots of help to accomplish what I set out to do.

The second type of resource is what the investing world calls "OPM," which stands for "other people's money." In other words, it is the ability to borrow funds in order to make more money. Here is a good example of this, say you came up with an idea of selling a bunch of candy bars at a baseball game, but you would need to buy a whole box to get the amount needed to sell them individually at the game for a profit. But you don't have any money for the purchase of the box. So you ask a friend who you know has extra money sitting in his piggy bank at home if he wants to partner with you by loaning you enough money to buy that box of candy bars. It is your duty to sell them, and once that's done, you split the profit with your money partner and give them back their original investment. You just made something out of nothing, and you created a win-win scenario for you and your partner. You made money off of his money by creating a system where you could use his funds to make a wise purchase that could be turned into a profit for both sides. That is exactly how it should work with borrowing money in the world of business and investing. You are leveraging yourself by borrowing additional funds from banks or other investors in order to have more buying power and to create a situation where you can double or triple your investing ability because now you have found a way to make money off of someone else's money. This is what I call smart business. You make your lender happy because you are literally growing their money for them with little to no effort on their part, and you are making more money than you could have had you invested with only your own money.

Even though I did have to borrow additional funds in order to make my first couple of real estate investment purchases, I could have opted to operate from that point on by using only my own cash and no longer borrow from others, but I would not have been able to buy as many properties within my desired timeframe. I could have still grown, but it would have been much slower. By continuing to borrow funds, I was able to buy double or sometimes even triple the properties than if I did it only using my own capital. I was able to make twice as much and grow twice as fast by learning how to properly use the bank and other people's money in order to make additional real estate investment purchases. That is how you leverage yourself when it comes to using debt in your business and investing ventures.

Robert Kiyosaki in his books also teaches the difference between bad debt and good debt. He says that bad debt, like personal credit cards and personal loans, takes money out of your pocket; whereas good debt, like real estate investments or a business loan, can potentially put extra money in your pocket. One loses you money, while the other provides you an opportunity to make you money. Understanding this very simple concept could be the difference between how well you do financially in your life and in your business versus how much you struggle to make it.

For me, learning to use other people's money to invest in my own business came somewhat naturally; however, learning to use other people to help me work in my business was a bit more of a challenge. With the financing portion of leverage, it truly is all about understanding basic math as it relates to money and knowing how to use those calculations to formulate a deal or a loan that will make you a profit or a return on your investment. But when it comes to the people portion of using leverage, it's a bit more complex. Learning to get along with and work with other people can be very challenging as everyone is so different. You can't treat everyone the same way because we all have different personalities and we each have our own way on how we like to do things or how we react to various situations as they come our way. In other words, there is no rulebook on how to handle working with a particular person; you just have to play it by ear for the most part.

By nature, I am the kind of person who would prefer to do something myself rather than tell someone else what it is exactly that I need or want done and when I expect it to be finished. I do not like waiting around for someone else to do something for me, especially if it is important and is costing me money. I like to be in control; however, part of allowing others the chance to do work for me is learning to let go of that control and trusting that even though I may not like how someone is doing a job or that they are taking longer than I expected, the job will get done eventually. I have to learn to be flexible to how others work or do things by at least giving them a fair chance to see a specific task through, then I can decide later if they are going to work out for my business long term or not. I usually factor that in by asking myself, "Is that person helping my business or hurting it?" I only want to work with people who are making a healthy contribution to what I'm trying to build as an entrepreneur; it's nothing personal; it's just how you have to be when trying to run and grow a successful business. Everyone has something to offer, but that does not mean they are the right fit for you. Leveraging people is about knowing how to best utilize someone's talent in a way that helps you accomplish more than you ever could on your own, and that's what it's all about.

So, figure out today how you can best leverage yourself to accomplish your own goals, whether it is in business or any aspect of your life. Like I said before, God has given us a world full of resources that are available to each and every single one of us; you just have to open your eyes a little wider, unlock your creative side, and get to work on building your pipeline. Levers can give you the power to accomplish some pretty remarkable and seemingly impossible things in this life; you just have to find yours and to not be afraid to use it.

NOTES

CHAPTER 17

Develop Patience

Probably one of the most difficult things I've had to learn as a real estate investor is learning to have patience, and to be honest, it is something I am still working on today. This is definitely something that has never really come natural for me, but I feel like my line of work has definitely forced me to improve in this area. If you can't be patient in real estate, then you are going to be in for some very long sleepless nights. Trust me, I know this from experience.

When I first started out, I wanted and expected things to happen right away; I did not like to wait very long for an answer or a result, especially when it came to my finances. I was always a bit of an aggressive risk-taker and very decisive when it came to investing money. Even as a young adult, it never took me very long to make big business decisions. But the problem with that aspect of my personality was that I did not like waiting. If I made an offer on a house or made any kind of business related proposal to anyone, I wanted an answer right then and there, not tomorrow or next week. I liked being in control, so I always had a hard time with not knowing and having to wait for an answer or for something to happen. In fact, that is my least favorite part of going to theme parks, shows, and driving in the city. I get bored very easily, so waiting can feel like torture at times.

With all of that being said, I have noticed that most young people are very much this way, but I also have noticed that as most people age they naturally start to become a little more patient over time. I suppose that has a lot to do with experience and just the fact that most people's lifestyles seem to slow down a bit as they get older. You know yourself a little better, and you've been around the block a few times, so the same types of situations that stressed you out when you're younger don't seem to bother you quite as much when you're older. This may not be true for everyone, but it seems to be the case with most, including myself, even though I consider myself to be pretty young still.

But for me, it has mostly been a heavy dose of experience in the patience department because of what I do for a living. I remember the very first house we fixed up and put on the market. I was excited and had high hopes of making my first profit in real estate, but at the same time, I was very anxious. I remember after having the house on the market for a couple of weeks and receiving no offer. I was calling my agent every other day or so, asking if he had an offer yet. He kept telling me he would call when one came in. After a month went by, we had dropped the price on the house more than once because I had over-priced it to begin with. I started to have major anxiety because the house was not selling and everything my wife and I had was tied up into that investment. It is scary flipping a house when you don't have or make a lot of money, and that was definitely the case for me at that time. Waiting for an offer to come in was driving me crazy, to the point to where I decided to hire a different agent hoping maybe that was the problem, but of course it wasn't the first agent's fault. We were in a very slow selling market, and the remodel we did was not all that great, being how it was my first time flipping a house. I finally accepted an offer after about three months on the market, even though it wasn't what I was hoping to get. However, I still made a decent profit, and now I could move on to my next flip.

When you are doing something kind of risky or hard for the first time, it can be very scary, you just have to approach it with an open mind. You have to understand that things might not work out quite like you were envisioning and probably won't happen within your planned timeline. You have to expect problems and delays because in almost every business deal or situation they are inevitable, and if you are expecting perfection, then you are going to be in for a wild emotional ride, especially if you are an impatient person.

Life is very much the same way. Rarely does anything ever actually go according to plan, and things always seem to take longer than they should. You just have to learn to go with the flow sometimes because there are a lot of things that are completely out of your control. You have to learn to be patient.

My next house flip was not any easier, and it was an even bigger test of my patience than the first. This time I received an offer right away, at the price I wanted, but an escrow that was supposed to take six weeks to close ended up taking over three months and almost fell out a couple of times, due to the fact that the buyers almost did not qualify for their loan. During this time, just as I had the first, I was growing very impatient and calling my agent and even the title company all the time because, like before, everything we had was tied up in this property and we were strapped for cash, even with my night job. I was very relieved when we closed on that one.

These two flips were probably my greatest test of patience because of the fact that I was just starting out and I was still very impatient at this time in my life. Since then, I have had several houses fall out of escrow, due to either the buyers not qualifying for financing, a negative inspection that scared potential buyers away, or simply the buyers changing their minds. It's tough when after all of the hard work it takes to fix up an entire house, plus so much time and money tied up into a project, you are subject to the mercy of one buyer or the bank who is giving them the funds to buy your house. I have had many sleepless nights stressing over lenders and underwriters who were giving us problems with qualifying one of our buyers or delaying an escrow by weeks. I learned very quickly that just because you have an accepted offer on a property does not guarantee a sale. It's not a done deal until you close escrow and the money is in your hands. I've seen too many deals fall apart due to this or that, and it hurts to have to put a house back on the market and deal with the lost time. In this business time really is money. There have been some properties that we opted to rent for a small period of time before finally being able to sell them for the price we needed to get. This also took great patience because you are basically getting a minimal return on your investment while you wait a year or so to collect your profit and original investment. Eventually, every house we have bought over the years with the intention to flip for a profit has sold, but boy did it take great perseverance on my part to wait those situations out.

Life will give you plenty of opportunities to learn patience; you just have to be able to not get too caught up in the race and recognize these learning moments as they come your way. I have to remind myself of this every time my patience is being pushed to the limits by a delayed project, sale, or escrow. Since I have never been able to talk to any of these mysterious underwriters of the various lenders that have held me up in escrow, I am 100 percent at their mercy, and all I can do sometimes is wait. All of the ranting and raving I do when things aren't going my way does me absolutely no good because it doesn't change a thing, but rather, it puts me in a state of depression and self-pity. When I get to that point, I just make things worse, so I've learned to wait patiently by distracting myself with positive things in my life. Doing this, I am much better off, and the waiting isn't nearly as painful for me.

Sometimes when you are not good at something, life will throw your weaknesses at you in ways that will either make it worse or force you to step up to the plate and face them head on until they become a strength. I have said this before, and I will say it again, there is no greater teacher in this life than experience. Some of life's greatest learning moments come in the form of hardship and adversity because these are the lessons we remember. When you are in the middle of turmoil and things appear hopeless or never ending, these are the times when you have to just hang on to some form of hope and learn how to persevere until it is over or resolved. When it comes to learning patience, it's important to stay focused on your long term goals and not get too hung up over every little bump in the road or delay. Remember that these things are all part of the journey we are each on. The other important thing to remember is that people are far from perfect, so they more than likely will let you down from time to time and in one way or another. Yes, you have to put your faith in people and trust that they will do what they say, but at the end of the day, the only person you can control is yourself. So it's important not to stress out too much or overreact when someone you have trusted lets you down. When this happens, do not allow yourself to lose complete faith in them or others because they might do much better next time around.

When you're in a position of leadership, it's important to be patient with those around you because you want them to return the favor when you mess up or let them down. We are all in this journey together, and none of us are perfect or get things right all of the time. Making mistakes is how we learn and grow, so be patient with those who you work with or that work for you. It might surprise you how much better they do next time, as long as they are fully aware of what they did wrong. You can inform them of this through positive reinforcement, rather than harsh criticism. The moment you lose faith in people is the moment when you will start to lose faith in yourself, and that can lead to deep depression, failed relationships, and low self-esteem, which is not a place where anyone wants to be. I believe we are in this world together to lift each other up when one of us is down, and I believe it starts with learning to be patient with one another.

Now, this can also include showing patience with yourself by not giving up so easily when you have failed to meet your own expectations. Just look at all of the failed attempts in the world of science; there are many accounts in our history of failed attempts that eventually led to great triumphs. Some of the greatest discoveries of mankind came after years and years of one failed attempt after another, until that person finally figured it out and got it right. Luckily, there have been many such people in Earth's history. They are examples of how great patience and perseverance can lead to remarkable accomplishments if we just learn to have faith in ourselves. Think about Thomas Edison and the lightbulb. But can you imagine any of these great inventors or heroes if they had given up on themselves after just a couple of tries? We certainly wouldn't have all of the luxuries and conveniences we all enjoy today. Someone had to be persistent and refuse to give up on their idea or their dream. Most importantly, they had to not give up on themselves.

So, now that we've discussed the importance of showing patience with people, how can we learn to be more patient with everyday circumstances or challenges? Well for starters, you need to first convince yourself that life is too short to worry and stress about all of the little things you simply cannot control. Second, realize that your personal happiness or self-worth has nothing to do with what goes on around you or what happens to you, but rather it is about how you respond and what you choose to do about it. There are just too many things in this life that we will never be able to fully control or manipulate to our liking or benefit, no matter how hard you try, so do your best and leave the rest up to fate. If you do that, things will always work out in the long run; the key is to never get so caught up in the moment that you lose sight of what matters most. This is a mindset that takes time to obtain, and that is why I believe patience is something we typically improve upon as we get older or as we gain more experience.

As I said before, when we are in the middle of these learning situations, it is important to distract yourself. So, do what you must to distract yourself while you are waiting for your moment or big pay day whatever that might be. What can you do or think about to help yourself remain positive? Remember, happiness is a choice, not something that happens to you. You can choose to be miserable by being negative and looking for things to complain about, or you can choose to be happy by waiting patiently by being positive, hopeful, and grateful for all of the good things in your life. I have found that grateful people are some of the happiest people, because they are always looking at the glass as half full, not half empty, and they don't allow negative things around them to tear them down or ruin their happiness.

So, make the choice today to be happy no matter what your circumstance may be because the situation won't last forever, but you will. You can't always control all of the things you will encounter on this journey called life, but you can most certainly decide how you will handle the journey, so make it a good one. Stop worrying about all of the things you can't control and start focusing on the things you can control. Everything else will sort itself out in the end, so try to enjoy the ride because it does go fast. If you do, your patience will start to come automatically, and you will be amazed by the results. So, hang in there, be patient, and remember that we are all in this race together.

NOTES

CHAPTER 18

Become Flexible

One thing I've learned about life and business is that things rarely ever go according to plan. It seems like there is always someone or something that gets in the way of whatever it is we are trying to accomplish or overcome, and if you can't learn to adjust to the sudden changes life will throw your way, then you are going to be in for some rude awakenings. I have seen many people who were so stuck in their way that despite numerous signs indicating that their way was wrong, they would persist in spinning their wheels and plugging away, going nowhere. But that's because that is how they've always done things, not realizing that there might be a better option. People may also act this way because they are scared to death of change and would rather be stuck in neutral the remainder of their lives than face the fear of stepping into the unknown, whether or not exploring new terrain could lead to a life of excitement and fulfillment. They are either too stubborn to admit they might be wrong, or they are too afraid to try anything new or different.

To some degree or another, I believe we have all fallen victim to one or both of these ways of thinking. Most people do not like change, and I don't know anyone who wants to admit that they might be wrong or that the old way is no longer the right way. We are all creatures of habit, and as such, we adopt certain behavioral patterns over time that define us in the way we handle or approach various situations that come our way, so much so that it can be difficult to change when needed. That is why it has been proven that the older we get, the harder it is to change and adjust to new surroundings. This is probably also one of the reasons why so often you see young kids teaching their grandparents how to use their smart phones or how to post things on Facebook. The evolution of technology has changed the way we do things as a society and the speed at which they are done. We live in a rapidly changing world, and if you can't keep up, then it's going to be tough to compete and succeed.

So, what does it take to overcome this way of thinking? The answer is "flexibility." To be flexible is to be willing to adapt to change by training yourself to adjust your previous way of thinking or doing things through learning a new and better way. This is not always an easy thing to do, especially if you are trying to change or unlearn a lifetime of a "this is how I've always done it" routine. Lifetime habits are for sure the hardest to break or bend, but this is a huge part of what it means to be flexible. You have to be willing to "go with the flow" or "roll with the punches" if you expect to not only keep up with society, but also be able to stay in the race for the long haul.

Let's take a look for a minute at the meaning behind the word flexible and why this word is used to describe someone who is willing to adjust to change. Let's take a bungee cord for example. If you were attempting to tie down a load in order to keep it from falling but were unsure of how much tie you would need to reach from one end to the other to ensure that your load stays secure, a bungee cord is great because it is able to change from its original length to a desired length. In other words, it is able to adjust as needed; therefore, it is helping you to keep your load nice and tight. Likewise, when we are being flexible, we are willing to expand our minds to the point that we are able to adjust to whatever life throws in our direction, whether it be a new state or tax law that affects how we are allowed to do business or a company that just moved into town that will be competing with you for business. It doesn't matter who you are or what you do for a living, everyone at some point in their lives will have to deal with change in one form or another. You can either choose to fight change by being stubborn or too scared to step into the unknown, or you can take the high road by embracing the inevitable and by making the necessary changes yourself that are required to succeed in whatever circumstance you find yourself in. Remember, like the bungee cord, we all have the ability to expand and adjust our way of thinking or doing things; we just have to be willing to put forth the effort to stretch until we reach our desired destination.

When I look back at my own journey and how I went from one starter home to owning over a dozen multi-family properties, I think of all the times I had to make adjustments with one new problem or difficult situation after another. All these situations enabled me to grow as a real estate company and as an investor. It wasn't easy; there were times when I wanted to give up or didn't think I had what it took to succeed because I felt like I didn't know what I was doing or that I simply wasn't smart enough. I grew up on a cattle ranch and struggled in school, and I hated doing construction. What business did I have as a young country guy and college dropout with no construction background trying to flip houses in a down market? Common sense told me I was crazy and that I should go find another job instead, and my old way of thinking was definitely trying to stop me from growing. It would have been so much easier to go back to being the person that gave up every time something looked impossible or felt uncomfortable. But I realized that the way I used to think wasn't working anymore, and if I wanted to be the person I dreamed of becoming, I knew I had to take a good long hard look at what changes I would need to make and find a way to adjust to a new and potentially better me. I would have to learn to be flexible because every house and every project brought its own unique set of challenges, and if I expected to succeed, then I had to be more open minded than I had ever been in my entire life. I had to be willing to learn a whole new world of real estate by treading in completely unfamiliar territory, and I had to be willing to adjust as required in order to excel at what I was doing.

I believe that this is something every new entrepreneur or business owner goes through when starting up something new and unfamiliar. It can be scary venturing out into the unknown, and you will have to make adjustments as changes come your way, but that is what keeps us always moving forward, rather than being stuck in neutral. As human beings, I believe it is our divine responsibility to always be striving to be a little better than we were yesterday, to not settle for mediocre but to seek progression, and to be willing to stretch when life calls for it. That to me is what it means to live a life of purpose and fulfillment.

As a real estate investor, I was given many opportunities to learn flexibility. I can remember one instance when we had bought this fancier house just outside of town, and it was nothing like the cheaper in town starter homes that I had gotten comfortable remodeling to sell. My brother-in-law, who was one of my partners, insisted that we go with nicer finishes and open the space up by removing walls, but I was feeling a little nervous because these changes would cost more money and take more time. We had done several flips up to that point and had done just fine doing thriftier, more basic remodels that took less time, but despite my fears and despite how we had successfully done previous flips, I knew he was right. Spending more money on a flip is always a gamble, but in the case of this particular house, it paid off. We made our biggest profit up to that point because we did it the right way. This house was nothing like the other starter homes that we had previously remodeled; it was a bigger, more luxurious home and in a better location, so our buyers would have higher expectations. This house even had its own tennis court with lights. If we had underdone the remodel, the results might not have been nearly as lucrative or successful. Sometimes it's important to recognize when change is needed because life and business will throw plenty of them at you, so pay attention and be ready to make the proper adjustments, so you can reap the benefits.

As my flipping career went on, the price of homes continued to rise, as did the cost of getting work done, so I had to constantly change and adjust the way I was doing these remodels in order to keep up with an ever changing real estate market. Buyers were getting pickier because the price of housing was going up, and inspectors were getting tougher due to the increase of construction because of an improving economy. So it was crucial that we improved the quality of our work and finishes by hiring the right guys and paying them more money to do the type of work that we needed them to do. The standard on remodeling houses had to improve if I was to keep up with the changes in the economy and if I wanted to stay in business. It was also imperative that I keep up with the changes in knowing what was trending or in other words what was in style. For example, when I started out, dark laminate floors were in style so were tile countertops, but now most everyone wants lighter laminate flooring because it lightens up the house and granite or quartz countertops because they are easier to keep clean; plus, it's a more expensive look.

When you are doing business, one of the most important things to remember is that the customer is always right because they are the ones who will decide what your product is worth to them and whether or not they will buy from you at all. If they like a certain product or style, then you better adjust because your success depends upon it. You can't get hung up on what you like or what you feel is best because you are not the one who is buying; you are the one selling, and if you don't cater to what the customer wants, then good luck making any sales. When I am making remodeling decisions and picking out finishes or colors, it is very important that I design the house according to what is currently most popular because that gives me the best chance to sell quicker and at the price I need in order to maximize profits. I have to give the buyers what they want, not what I want.

A lot of business owners really struggle with this concept, especially in the house flipping business. They get emotionally attached to the house they're fixing up or get too hung up on what used to be popular, forgetting that it's a business and that in order to succeed you have to do what's most beneficial or desirable to your potential buyer. I never had a problem with getting attached because I wanted to see that house sell as quickly as possible, so I could collect my profit sooner and move on to the next project. In fact, I used that same mentality in my marketing strategy. I have always tried to treat my house flipping as a cash flow business, and I have done that by being willing to adjust my expectations from time to time by doing whatever it took to make a sale. This is another example of how I had to learn to be flexible in order to keep my business going strong. I usually sold a house for a little less than it appraised for, so I could sell it quicker, and I never got too stuck on getting the highest price possible during a negotiation with a buyer because I wanted to get that property in escrow, so I could keep things moving forward.

I call this the Walmart mentality. It's true that Walmart sells their products cheaper than most of their competition, but they also have way more sales than anyone else, other than maybe Amazon, who also follows the same pattern of product pricing but does so on online. Because of this fact, they are by far the biggest brick and mortar retail chain in the world.

One last example I want to share from personal experience about learning to be flexible is when I made the decision to start acquiring rental properties a little earlier than originally planned. House flipping, when done right, yields a much higher return on investment than holding properties for rental income, so it made sense to flip houses for as long as possible before putting some of that money into a steady long term investment, like rental properties. The problem was, I had quit my job, so I had no steady income and the house flipping business is very feast or famine. By our third year in, we had gotten up to seven houses; this includes either houses being remodeled, on the market, or in escrow. I was trying to grow as fast as possible, so I had invested everything I had, leaving very little to live off of with no real stream of income. So, if a house didn't sell, I was in trouble. Well, that was exactly what happened, call it bad luck or call it a coincidence, but none of our houses were scheduled to close for several months and several remodels went over budget, so I had to not only borrow additional funds to finish a project, but I also had to borrow funds to live off of while waiting for something to close in escrow. A house would sit on the market with no offers, a buyer would back out for this reason or that, or our buyer would struggle to qualify for financing, so escrow would be delayed for weeks. Even though we came out on the other end making a lot of money because the houses did eventually sell, it was financial survival trying to get through those few months with no income and being over extended. Yes, I realized that was the risk I took as an entrepreneur, but it felt a little too risky. I knew I could not keep doing business like that, so that's when we took part of the money and decided to start buying multi-family properties that would serve as steady income while we waited for houses to close to cash out on our flips. Rental properties would also serve as a means to help pay business bills as they came along; besides the remodels themselves, it cost money to hold on to vacant houses. So, that was what we did, and it worked out like a charm in the long run. We turned one business into two. The house-flipping business would provide the better return for the short run, and the rental business would be a smaller return but provide a steady long term cash flow that we desperately needed.

The two businesses worked side by side, each serving their own purpose yet supporting one another as well. By acquiring rental properties while flipping houses, we were also able to amass a ton of equity because the value of our properties would increase over time, so our net worth went up as the market did, and our tenants' rent would be paying down our loans for us. On top of all that, rental properties are great tax shelters for other types of income as well, like our flipping business. These are some of the hidden financial benefits to owning rentals; the real estate world calls this "phantom cash flow." This was all made possible because I was willing to set aside my ego of trying to chase better returns by only flipping and by deciding to be smart and to diversify our business through investing in long term multifamily properties a little earlier than originally planned. It was a slower growing plan from that point on, but it put us in a much better position be able to stay in business for the long haul, and it definitely made my wife feel a lot better, knowing that we had some form of cash flow coming in while waiting for houses to close. I hope that by sharing these stories of how I benefited from learning to be flexible to changes and curve-balls that continuously hit my business that you can learn from these examples and use these lessons to help you in your own business or personal pursuits.

So, what are the things that are holding you back from making the necessary changes that you need to make in order to take your business to the next level? Is it pride, or is it fear? Both can keep you from having the humility or the courage to make the necessary adjustments to overcome obstacles as they appear before you. When it comes to your business or your personal life, if you don't learn to roll with the punches or go with the flow and you choose to fight change rather than embrace it, you will find it very difficult to grow as an individual, and you will miss out on many of the possibilities this life has to offer.

Learning to be flexible is something that we all must learn to do if we want to sustain success and hold onto it for the long run. Doing this is also essential to our progression and personal growth as an entrepreneur or a person, and that is what I believe is what this life is truly all about. Change is inevitable, and we are all subject to it, so why not make it work for you, rather than against you, by being flexible?

NOTES

CHAPTER 19

Learn Accountability

ONE THING I'VE NOTICED about most people is, when something doesn't go right in their life, it seems to be their natural reaction to look for someone or something to blame for their predicament. They blame the world for their problems and forget to look in the mirror. They love to complain about all of the people who did them wrong or all of the bad luck that seems to follow them around, but they refuse to admit that they might be the cause behind whatever it is that is going wrong in their life. As human beings, we hate being wrong, and we especially hate it when somebody else points out our mistakes. But the fact is, we all make mistakes, all of the time, whether we like admitting it or not, and the only way we improve and overcome these mistakes is by recognizing our faults. We have to be willing to admit to ourselves and those around us, if necessary, when we have messed up. This is called being accountable, and I have found this character trait to be one of the most important traits we can possess when pursuing the path to a successful mindset, especially if you are an entrepreneur or aspiring to become one.

I believe the main purpose of this life is to progress and become better than we were. The only way we can do this is by acknowledging our weaknesses and by admitting when we have made a mistake or when we have fallen short of being the person we know we are capable of being. This takes great humility because you are literally letting your guard down by setting aside your pride and by choosing to be teachable. Life has so many wonderful things it wants to teach us, but until we reach the point of accountability, we will never be able to truly allow ourselves the opportunity to learn and grow the way we are capable of doing. I have noticed that life tends to give us each our own unique set of obstacles or trials that are meant just for us, but we are the ones who have to make the choice of whether or not we will learn the lesson that is there for us to learn. I believe that many of these obstacles are placed in our path because of a chain reaction that has resulted from poor choices we have made throughout our life. In other words, many of our problems come from our own doing—not someone or something else.

When I was starting out in the cattle business just a couple of years after high school, I started buying feeder calves with the sole intention of getting

CHAPTER 19: Learn Accountability

them up to certain size, then selling them for a profit. The problem was that I was buying them too young and at the wrong time of the year. I was buying 300-pound feeder calves that were taken away from their mothers too soon and expecting them to do well on hay, rather than grain and fresh grass. I was also buying them just before winter, so the cold, wet weather did not help my cause. I was buying them young because they were much cheaper, and I was more focused on building up a higher number of cattle, rather than focusing on buying them at the right size and feeding them the right way. My theory was quantity, not quality. Hay is fine for bigger cattle, but it just doesn't have all of the proper nutrients that younger feeder calves need to grow the way they should in order to do well; plus, young calves off of milk in the winter is usually a bad combination because they get sick pretty easy and the chances of them dying increase. But, being the young inexperienced, yet overly ambitious entrepreneur, that I was, I just kept buying cattle that I felt were most affordable without really thinking things through as well as I should have. I thought I was making good deals because I was buying cheap, but unfortunately, it turned out to be one mistake after another. I ended up paying the price for those mistakes in buying feeder calves so young and during the wrong time of year. One winter, I lost about 20 percent of my little herd, and the ones that did survive did not do very well at all. They did not grow like I expected or hoped they would, so I had to hold onto them much longer than originally intended, which resulted in me not making very much money due to having to buy extra feed and losing time. I actually ended up losing more than I made. Luckily for me, at the time I was still living at home with no family to support, so I was able to afford to make those kinds of business mistakes, but it definitely slowed down my progression in building up my dream herd and being a successful cattle investor.

Furthermore, losing your hard-earned money always hurts. Every time I lost an animal back then, it hurt because I was losing several hundred dollars and that was a big deal because I didn't have a whole lot of money when I was first starting out. The hardest part, besides losing money, was that I had to admit to myself that the way I was buying cattle was wrong, and if I wanted to make money in that business, I would need to stop being so cheap, to buy older better quality cattle, and to make sure they were getting fed the right way.

Like a lot of young business owners starting out, there was a lot of trial and error with learning what was a good buy and what was not, but the most important lesson I learned was admitting that what I was doing was simply not working. I realized that if I wanted to succeed, I needed to change my methods. I had to hold myself accountable for my own mistakes. I could have blamed the market, the weather, or bad luck, but at the end of the day, I was the one making the decisions, so I realized that I was the one who needed to change and start doing things differently if I was to expect better results for next time. Admitting you're wrong is never an easy thing to do, but it is necessary if you want to grow as an individual or if you expect your business to succeed.

We all make mistakes; the important thing is how you choose to respond afterwards. Do you choose to correct your mistakes by making a change or by finding a better way to do something, or are you going to choose to be stubborn and continue doing the same thing expecting a different outcome? The latter option is defined as "insanity," which is basically doing the same thing over and over again, expecting a different result. You may know someone who fits this model of behavior, or it might even describe the way you have handled a situation in the past. Either way, we all know that refusing to change something, even when all signs are telling us that it is not working, is silly. It's like beating your head against a wall.

Going back to the story I told earlier about my first ever attempt at investing in real estate, after having failed in the cattle business I was over anxious to prove to myself and to those around me that I could make it as an entrepreneur and that I wasn't a failure. This caused me to dive head first into a business I knew nothing about by purchasing a property clear across the country without ever even having visited the area of Flint, Michigan or seeing the house in person. I really convinced myself at the time that I could get rich quickly by simply finding good deals online without doing proper research, then flipping them to someone else for a profit without doing any repairs or improvements to the property whatsoever. Like I mentioned

CHAPTER 19: Learn Accountability

earlier, I ended up losing money on that deal and coming to the realization that it wasn't going to be as easy as I thought and that if I was going to be successful in real estate, I would be required to do more research on the subject and save more money, so that I could afford to buy homes locally. I learned that there are all types of real estate markets, and that not all of them are smart to invest in. Also, if you want to truly increase the value of something, you have to find ways to actually physically improve your product in one way or another. Most importantly, I learned that if something seems too easy or too good to be true, then it probably is. If you want to be successful at anything in this life, whether in your business or personal life, I suggest you don't take the bait luring you towards the easier, quicker path, but rather take the path that seems more realistic and doable but will require more effort on your part. You will be grateful you did so in the long run.

Not only will the more difficult path probably be the more achievable between the two, but it will also be the path that forces you to learn and grow the most. I had to be accountable for my mistake, just like I did in buying the wrong type of cattle prior to then and admit that I definitely jumped the gun by allowing my ego and unrealistic dreams to get in the way of common sense. I learned that real estate is not just something you can stumble or dive into without educating yourself the right way first and that you have to be in it for the long term if you are to be successful. Just like anything else, you have to do it in steps, and if you try skipping any steps, you will find that you're building a house of cards, rather than something that is going to last and see you through the tough times. Even though I never made the same mistake again of buying a house sight unseen in a place where I had never been before again, I still found myself making rash decisions early on as a real estate investor, which led to losing precious time and potential profit. But in all fairness, I was new to the world of house flipping and construction, so I was figuring things out as they came my way. I learned a lot from each money costing mistake I made, and you can't teach experience. But what made me have the ability to turn each failure into a learning opportunity was the willingness to accept my weaknesses and inexperience by taking accountability for all of my actions. When something would go wrong, rather than point the finger at a contractor, real estate agent, or an inspector, I would put the blame on myself and that would force me to do whatever it took to improve the situation and do better next time. After all, when you own a business, you are the one held responsible when things don't go according to plan, and you are the one who is expected to make it right. This is something I had to learn early on in my first couple of years investing in fixer upper houses in order to be successful at it.

Looking back, I realize now how unrealistic my dreams of getting rich quickly without much effort really were. I know now that for most of us, if you want to be successful at anything in life, especially business, you have to work hard for it. I wanted to make it big by doing something that required very little effort or time; that's why my dreams were unrealistic: it was the way I wanted to achieve them.

So it would be a year or so before making another attempt at real estate investing, but this time I would do it the right way. I bought a house undervalued and in my area, and this time not only did I do my research and prepare myself with information, but I went into the project intending to upgrade the property by remodeling it, rather than turning around to sell it the way I bought it. I chose to put in the extra time, money, and work by physically improving the value of the property. The results were much different this time; I actually made money and the rest is history.

The important lesson here is that I once again had to swallow my pride, admit that I was wrong, and make a change. I had to completely alter the way I had originally planned and thought I was going to make money in the field of real estate investing. I had to own up to my mistake by admitting that I was wrong and showing that I was humble enough to go back to the drawing board, deciding to take the time to properly learn something before plunging into it. I also couldn't blame anything or anyone but myself and my impatience; it was my fault for trying to make a quick buck by doing something I knew very little about.

This is what it means to be accountable, to recognize or admit when you've made a mistake. Don't blame others; admit your mistake, and do what you can to correct it or make it better.

I would like to discuss again, briefly, about why it's so important that we be willing to take the fall when we fail at something, versus looking for someone else to blame. Like I mentioned earlier, it is human nature to complain when things aren't going our way and to look to pin our problems on a cause outside of ourselves. Why do we do this? It's very simple: nobody likes admitting their faults. It feels better to have an excuse or a good reason for our failures and shortcomings, doesn't it? If we blame ourselves, then we are admitting that we fell short and that we made a mistake. We are also admitting that we may not know quite as much as we thought we did and that, just maybe, we are not quite as good as we thought we were. It humbles us and reminds us that we have much to learn. Nobody likes to be humbled, especially when we live in a society that preaches self-pride. While yes, it is important to have some pride in what you do and who you are, it is also important to be humble enough to admit when you are wrong or when you need to make a change. That is how we learn, and that is how we grow.

Nobody is born knowing everything; we learn from trial and error. But it all starts with taking accountability for your actions, being willing to take the fall even if it's easier or less painful to pin the blame on something else. That is one of the things that separates a good leader from everyone else or a good business owner from an employee. A good leader and business owner is willing to take the blame when things go wrong. They are willing to be accountable when everyone else is looking for someone or something to blame. They are willing to take the fall, even if it means setting aside their pride and ego. They do it because that is how they improve and that is how they overcome.

There is one more aspect of accountability that I want to discuss before concluding this chapter, and that is learning when to quit or walk away. This is something a lot of investors struggle with, especially those who are passive or inexperienced investors. Let's use gambling as an example. Say you walk into a casino with the intention of only allowing yourself to lose a set amount of money. You find a slot machine and begin pulling the handle. You make money right out the gate, giving you hope of actually walking away from the casino with more than what you came in with. Then suddenly, you start to lose what you won, and before you know it, you find yourself losing more and more. What do you do? Do you keep chasing that hope of making money where most do not by continuing to gamble, or do you walk away and stop the bleeding before it gets any worse? The same could be said for an investor who puts his money into a stock that they thought was destined for success. Despite their efforts, they realize that the stock is plummeting in value right before their very eyes, and they now have two choices. They can leave it there in hopes that things will turn around soon, or they can cut their losses and pull their money out before they lose it all. Both of these examples show that there are major risks when putting your money into a slot machine or in the stock market, but, more importantly, they test the gambler or investor to see at what point they are willing to stop what they are doing once they realize they are losing and maybe headed for financial disaster.

Real estate can be very much the same way if you're not careful. A bad property purchase or a sudden down turn in the market can put you in a position where you either sell now and take your losses or hold out in hopes for a miracle turn around and maybe lose a ton more. I can go on and on with examples about how sometimes it's wise to realize when something isn't working like we thought it would and to pull out while we still can before we lose anymore. It doesn't take a genius to recognize when something isn't working out like expected, but it does take courage and great will power sometimes to walk away. Once again, you have to be willing to set your pride or ego aside and know when to say, "Enough is enough." This is another part of learning to be accountable for your actions and learning to be a true leader when everyone else is looking to play the blame game. So stop and think about all of the times that you have had to walk away from something or have had to admit when you were wrong. Now think of how you can learn from those times, so that you are prepared for whatever the future has in store for you because life will give you plenty of opportunities to learn accountability.

So, step up to the plate and don't be afraid to admit when you are wrong. Have the courage to face the truth, rather than running or hiding from it, pretending it doesn't exist, or thinking that things will just magically start falling into place. Things rarely sort themselves out or change on their own. You have to be willing to adjust and make that change happen, but it starts with you recognizing this fact and doing something about it. It starts with you being accountable for your actions and accountable for your life!

NOTES

CHAPTER 20

Be Focused

THERE IS A QUOTE that I like by Alexander Graham Bell, the Scottish-American scientist and inventor of the first practical telephone, that goes, "Concentrate all your thoughts upon the work at hand. The sun's rays do not burn until brought to focus." When I first heard this quote, I tried to find the deep meaning behind it, and I came to the conclusion that anything we accomplish in life, whether it be building a successful business or earning your very first paycheck, takes focus. The ability to focus on our goal determines results or the level of outcome. Whether we are young or old, male or female, rich or poor, we all want to live happy and successful lives. But the one thing that separates those who come out successful in this pursuit versus those who fall short is a person's level of determination and focus.

If you want something bad enough and it is within your ability or potential to achieve, then the only person at the end of the day that can actually stop you is yourself. While it is true that some are born more privileged than others and some are more gifted when it comes to talent and ability, we all have the equal opportunity to decide how hard we try and how far we are willing to push ourselves. But this all starts with having the desire to be successful and the will power to do whatever it takes to get there. Sure, there will always be difficult road blocks and unforeseen obstacles that will get in our way and try to hinder our pursuit of success, but if we stay the course and persevere with the resources made available to us, we can do anything we set our minds to do.

The last part of Alexander Bell's quote is intriguing because he uses the analogy of the power of the sun and explains how its potential to burn is not enough. It is not the rays themselves, but it is the focus of the rays that has such a powerful effect on everything they touch. Likewise, we as individuals have each been given gifts and abilities that give us the potential to do great things, but if we don't learn to focus our efforts in making them work for us, then all of that power becomes useless and ineffective. We become like a candle with no flame or a flashlight with no batteries. Potential alone is not enough to cultivate success; you have to light that flame within yourself if you want to see and feel the results of its brightness and warmth. The way you do this is to focus your energy by using your God-given tal-

CHAPTER 20: Be Focused

ents to take action on going after the things you want to accomplish in life and by being persistent in your pursuits. Be focused on the big things, as well as the small. Continue to do all of the everyday little things that move you closer to accomplishing your goals.

I am a huge sports fan, and my favorite athlete and player to watch as a kid was the famous Michael Jordan, winner of six NBA Championships and arguably the greatest basketball player, maybe even greatest athlete, of our time. Besides his many God-given talents, he clearly displayed focus on the court, and it was this focus that really separated him from everyone else and allowed him to excel when it really mattered. He was intent on putting all his efforts into doing whatever it took to winning games and being the best in the business. He literally left it all on the court, leaving no room for excuses or a lack of effort, and because of this, he wowed us all with his brilliant performances and basketball resume. Michael Jordan also set a powerful example for the rising generation on what it means to really give it your all and to not let your talents go to waste through laziness and self-doubt. He demonstrated having a laser focus and never giving up on your dreams or, especially, on yourself. So, what idols did you have growing up that inspired you to be the best version of yourself and made you believe that anything is possible if you set your mind to it?

Growing up in a religious environment, I was taught that we are the children of a loving God and have all been blessed with our own unique set of talents. Because of this, we all have the potential to be great if we learn to use these talents to help improve not only our lives, but the lives of those around us. I was taught that we are expected to be wise with what we have been given by not letting it go to waste, and as I've gotten older, I've learned that when you make the effort to focus on what you really want out of life, you are able to magnify your abilities and gifts and, more importantly, what you choose to do with them.

Another aspect of being focused is learning to stay engaged in what is going on around you. This was not always a strong suit for me, and being focused is something I have had to develop overtime, like most everything else. When I was in early grade school, my teachers used to give me a hard time for not paying attention. I was a bit of a daydreamer, so sitting there in a classroom for several hours trying to focus in on everything that was being taught was not my forte. I preferred being outside, doing hands-on activities not being stuck in a room, listening to adults talk about stuff I could care less about. I can remember once getting sent to the principal's office, and it was brought up that they wanted to diagnose me with ADD (Attention Deficit Disorder). However, my parents must have intervened because they never actually went through with it. (I think labeling kids when it is not absolutely necessary is one of the worst things you can do as a teacher or a mentor because it defeats them and destroys their self-confidence. Every time they make a mistake, they will blame it on whatever they were labeled with earlier in their life and use it as a reason for not trying something new or challenging.) As I got older though, I started to find subjects I enjoyed learning about, and I also started to figure out how to focus better on things being taught in classroom settings, even though I still, to this day, am much better at learning outside the classroom.

One way that helped me become more engaged was regularly participating in discussions rather than just sitting there staring quietly. Although it was still a struggle to sit there and try to listen in class, I found that the more I actively involved myself by participating as much as I could, the more I was able to keep myself in tune to what was going on around me, rather than being lost in my own little universe. Once I realized that I was a hands-on learner, I was able to excel where I needed to in my school years, and ultimately, that prepared me to becoming a successful entrepreneur and business owner. But it all started with discovering what method worked best for me and also figuring out how I learned best, so that I could focus in on what I was doing or trying to accomplish at the time and not allow myself to be distracted by my day dreaming.

Becoming a good listener is also an important component when it comes to being focused. It is important to learn how to be a good listener, even if you are not interested in what is being said or taught, because if you expect people to listen to what you have to say, you need to be able to return them the favor by respecting what they have to say. It goes both ways. This idea definitely applies to marriage or a business partnership. If you want your relationship to last and be successful, then it is vital that you learn to treat your partner with respect by being a good listener and showing interest in how the other side may feel about something

Being focused is not just about harnessing your potential and learning to pay attention, it is also about have your eyes and mind fixated on something so strongly that no outside noise or influence can distract you from accomplishing your task at hand. There is another quote about being focused that I like by a Brazilian novelist named Paulo Coelho: "Whenever you want to achieve something, keep your eyes open, concentrate and make sure you know exactly what it is you want." I can't express enough how important it is to have vision when it comes to pursuing a successful mindset and a life of fulfillment. To have vision, as it pertains to focus, is to know what it is you want out of life and to know who you want to be in this life. Once you have a vision, you then need to have the willingness to do whatever it takes to make that happen. It means to have a dream, then to follow up by taking the necessary steps of action and doing everything within your power to make that dream a reality. Ask any self-made millionaire entrepreneur or famous entertainer, and he or she will tell you that before all of the success they had a dream and a belief in their ability to fulfill that dream; when they pursued that dream, they never gave up on themselves. Every great accomplishment in the history of our world started out as one tiny idea that grew and grew until eventually blossomed into something spectacular.

I have always loved the analogy of comparing anything success related to planting a seed. It's very small when starting out, but if planted in good soil and properly nourished every day throughout its life, one day that seed will transform into a beautiful tree for all to enjoy and benefit from. But it takes patience, effort, and consistency in order to make this miraculous transformation a reality or a possibility. The same goes with each one of us. When starting out in life, we may feel very small, but once we realize our true potential and start doing all of the little everyday things needed for our growth, we will start to notice a transformation in ourselves. We will start to see ourselves changing into the person we always knew deep down inside we were capable of becoming, but it takes persevering and enduring to the end. It takes you focusing each and every single day on taking one step after another until eventually your dream becomes a reality. Most importantly, it takes never giving up on yourself.

So what is it that you want? When starting out in life, I believe that most of us had a pretty good idea of what we wanted out of this world and what we expected from ourselves. But somehow, life seems to have a way of trying to drag us down by beating us up with trials and challenges and making us feel like our dreams of success are either not realistic or simply out of reach. We allow failure and imperfection to define us by telling us what we can or can't do, thus putting an end to any real growth in our lives. We allow life to distract us from achieving our dreams and reaching our potential because we lost focus somewhere along the line on what matters most to us. Don't let this happen to you. If you are not at all where you expected or hoped to be by this point in your life, then stop and take a long, hard moment to reflect back on where things might have gone wrong, so that you can do something today to change your outcome for tomorrow.

It is never too late to take positive action in your life, and when it comes down to it, we are truly the only ones who can limit how far we go. There will be many things on our life's journey and pursuit of success that will try to distract us or discourage us from trying to reach our goals. It is up to us to figure out how to overcome them, so we don't let them derail us from getting to where we want to get and becoming who we want to be.

Here are a few tips that have helped me to stay on track in my own business venture and have helped me to keep moving forward, even when things seemed to be coming to a crashing halt. The first is to write down your goals and what you would like to accomplish over the next few years, then review them at least once a month to make sure you are indeed staying the course. It is okay if you don't meet every goal; just be sure you don't stop striving to get there eventually. Second, come up with a plan on how you will accomplish your goals, as this helps you make them a reality not a wish list. Get this plan in writing as well and review it along with your goals each and every month to make sure your sticking to it. Be open to adjusting your plan as needed, as life will sometimes force you to do so, but don't waiver from taking the necessary steps that will move you closer to where you want to end up. Third, come up with a successful, yet doable, daily routine that will help you develop winning habits on your road to a better you and a better life. Remember it's not about the big life changing moments that define you, but rather, it is all of the little daily actions that you choose to make or not make that decide who you are. Fourth, find a way to drown out the noise because life will bring you plenty of distractions to get you off track and off target, causing you to lose focus on what's important. Do things to keep you motivated, like listening to inspiring music or reading inspiring books. Try to avoid negativity and anyone or anything that might drag you down or make you feel like you're not good enough. Find things that build you up, not tear you down. Fifth, find your why and never let it out of your mind. See the dream or the pot of gold at the end of the rainbow as if it was a reality today, and hold it close to you at all times. Constantly remind yourself why you are doing all of this, and keep telling yourself that it is all worth it because it is. If you practice these five things I promise you that nothing can stop you from getting to where you want to get in life and from becoming who you know deep down inside you were destined to become.

So, get started if you haven't already, and do whatever it takes to stay focused on your dreams and stay focused on the destination. Never take your eyes off of the prize because that is the one thing that will keep you motivated to never give up and endure to the end.

NOTES

CHAPTER 21

Show Integrity

When it comes to personal conduct, there are two basic ways of doing business, honestly and dishonestly. Let me break this down a bit, and I'll explain these two very different approaches because they apply to everything we do in life, not only in how we do business.

To be honest means to always be truthful in everything you do, big or small. It doesn't matter if it's one dollar or a thousand dollars, you treat it the same because you want to be fair with people and only take what belongs to you or what you agreed upon, nothing more. It also means being a man or a woman of your word. When you tell someone that you're going to do something, you do it. If for whatever reason you can't fulfill your promises to someone, you don't try to ignore it or make up excuses, but you take accountability and tell them the truth. Trust me even if it means being vulnerable, people will respect you a whole lot more if you tell the truth and are being honest with them in everything. In business, trust is everything.

Being honest also means not cheating, even if you don't feel like it's hurting anyone else. When you cheat in anything, the only person you are really hurting in the long run is yourself. When you cheat, you are trying to get something you don't deserve or didn't earn without putting in the required effort it takes to get whatever it is you're after. You are basically trying to get something for nothing, which seems like a great idea in the short term, but it hurts you long term because when you cheat to get through you are depriving yourself of actually learning anything and you will never grow as a person, which is the whole purpose of this life. The greatest wealth we can obtain from this world isn't in seeing how many material things we can accumulate or how much fun we can have; it is building strong relationships and progressing as an individual. It is about obtaining knowledge through experience and hard work. People who only care about making as much money as possible and having as many nice things as they can possibly obtain in their life but don't care who they have to step on to get these things are not showing integrity. The only thing that matters to them is getting what they want. But when you are showing true integrity, you care about the needs of those around you, and you do everything in your power to make sure their needs are being met, as well as your own. You strive always to be honest and fair in all of your dealings both in your personal life and in your business. You don't take what is not rightfully yours; you don't lie to get ahead or to avoid looking vulnerable, and you don't cheat yourself by trying to get something for nothing. You are not only being honest with your fellowman but you are also being honest with yourself.

Now, on the flip side, you have dishonesty. To be dishonest means to deceive in one way or another, and it is broken down into three basic categories: lying, stealing, and cheating. All three of these things are a basic makeup of what exactly it means to be dishonest, but it can get quite confusing when it comes to business because there are many gray areas when it comes to this subject.

What do I mean by gray areas? Well, let me give you an example. Say you are selling a product, and the customer accidentally over pays you by a few dollars; neither one of you catches the mistake at first, but later that day you notice that they paid you too much; however, they are now long gone. Fortunately, you have their information, so you have a means of tracking them down, but they have no clue and will probably never say anything. It's only a few bucks, so part of you feels that it's not a big deal and you can use all the extra cash you can get because you plan to do great things with your business. But the other part of you realizes that, while yes, it's not a whole lot, but the fact is that technically it is still being dishonest because you were paid more than what you agreed. This is what I call I moral dilemma. You are faced with the decision to either let one little dishonest act go or step up and make the decision to make it right by correcting the mistake and being completely honest. Many people in a situation like this would find several justifications to keep the money and convince themselves that it's not a big deal, so why make it one? After all, it isn't a lot of money, and they don't even know about it or seem to care. In business, these types of small moral dilemmas happen all the time, and they are considered gray areas because, while yes, technically you're being a little dishonest if you don't act, it's not a lot and your intentions were never to rip anybody off. The problem with letting something like this slide is that it becomes easier and easier to repeat in future business dealings, thus becoming a slippery slope for you and your business. Being dishonest about little things can become habit-forming until, eventually, you start justifying being dishonest about much bigger things.

This is where the word integrity kicks in. If someone can't trust you, then why in the world would they want to do business with you? That goes for a business partner, employee, contractor, client, customer, or even a lender. We all want to be assured that the person we are entrusting our financial lives over to is an honest person and someone we can trust to treat us fairly at the end of the day.

It's easy to be honest when everyone is looking, but what about when nobody is watching? Are you still the same person, or do you let your guard down by taking the easy way out and practice integrity only when you have something to gain? Remember, true integrity is being honest at all times no matter what the situation is, not just when it's most convenient. I have always been a very honest person, but like everyone else, that honesty has been put to the test many times, especially when doing business.

Because of how I grew up and having great examples before me on not being wasteful and living on a budget, I have always been very thrifty by nature. I have never liked spending more money than I have to, and I have always been very careful with my spending habits. I was taught from a very young age the importance of putting money away and never spending more than you make. I was also taught how to negotiate prices and the importance of being a bargain hunter. If it's not on sale, don't buy unless you absolutely have to. The only problem with having this mentality is that you tend to take every opportunity or chance you get to save money, even if that means trying to cut corners in order to save.

Once I got into real estate, I knew that in the beginning I would need to hire experts to help me remodel these properties I was buying at discount prices. In order to make a profit, I would have to put my smart money skills to use by being thrifty and watching my spending. But sometimes I would be tempted to be too cheap with how I did things, cutting corners during the remodel in order to save time and money. Now, when it came to paying the guys, I was very good about paying them whatever they charged so long as it was fair, but once we agreed on price, I always paid the full amount I owed them and on the time we agreed upon. I knew the importance of being honest with people who were working hard for me, and I hated owing someone money, so I always paid my bills on time. But during these earlier remodels, I would sometimes be tempted to try and hide things that might potentially be a problem for a buyer later on down the road. This is, in fact, one of the negative stereotypes about house flippers, that we remodel for as cheaply as possible, so we leave more room for a bigger profit and that we try to hide everything with paint, carpet, and trim. Obviously not every house flipper thinks or works like this, because if they did, they wouldn't stay in business for long. The shady work will catch up to you eventually. But when I started out, I didn't have a lot of money or know much about construction, so I definitely cut corners that probably I shouldn't have. It was never intentional because I really didn't know what I was doing in the beginning. However, as I started figuring out the do's and don'ts of construction, I definitely started running into moral dilemmas regarding decisions on how to fix something properly for more money versus covering it for less money.

I can honestly say that as an entrepreneur I have always strived to take the higher road when it came to doing the right thing in business because it has always been in my DNA and makeup as a person to always try to do the right thing, even if it cost me some of my profit. I always felt that if I wanted stay in business for the long run, I had to do so fixing things the right way, and if I wanted to have a peace of mind and sleep well at nights knowing I am being honest, then I better strive to have the work done the way it should be done. It took me some time to get comfortable with this concept because I hated spending too much money on anything, but it was the right choice, and it helped me stay in business. Furthermore, it helped me to become an even better person. I always made enough; I didn't need to be deceitful by being too cheap and cutting corners that shouldn't be cut. With flipping houses, you have to find that balance between not being careless by overspending yet not being too cheap by underspending. The most important thing is that you don't try to deceive your buyers by selling them something you didn't fix up the right way. That is one of the ways that I learned the importance of being honest in my business dealings and showing business integrity.

Money comes and goes, but the way you treat others and the relationships you can cultivate by doing so can last forever. Without trust you are like a ship without a sail or a car without a steering wheel; you might survive for a little while, but eventually a turn or current will come that you didn't expect, and you will be in for a disastrous outcome. Trying to get ahead by being deceitful is just as bad as trying to get ahead by stepping on others—in fact, it might even be worse. At least when you are not hiding your horrible behavior and selfish actions, people see you coming and have a chance to react, but when you cheat someone by stabbing them in the back, they don't even see you coming, so they don't have a fighting chance. Sure, getting victories this way might seem satisfying in the moment, but sooner or later, cheating your way to the top will catch up to you, and it will not be as pleasant as it once was. We all have to pay the price for are misdeeds, whether immediately or further down the road, and if we don't correct them now, it will cause a disastrous end to our journey. This leads to the opposite of a successful life.

It's not about getting there as fast as possible and doing whatever it takes to get there; it's about getting there the right way, so when you arrive at your destination, you actually have the ability to stay there. That means you can feel proud of yourself and the journey you took to become successful. Integrity is what will bring us true happiness and satisfaction at the end of the day. You can build success without having to lie, cheat, or steal, and doing so allows you to build up a reputation of being honest and showing integrity.

NOTES

CHAPTER 22

Learn Humility

I HAVE LISTED many ways you can achieve business and personal success through obtaining a successful mindset, but there is one important attribute that many of us tend to forget about—being humble. I see a lot of people who, once they start getting a taste of authority or financial success, forget where they came from and start thinking they are better than other people, although some of them may never admit it out loud. They let success get to their heads and feel that they can't possibly do wrong. They become way too prideful, which can be a scary place because that can lead to making irrational decisions or refusing to admit when you are wrong. When you become overconfident in yourself, you lose the ability to be teachable or flexible when life throws new and unexpected challenges your way. Pride can also lead to selfishness, which can turn you into the type person that other people do not want to work with because either they can't trust you or they feel like you don't really care about them.

I believe that pride is very much connected to greed; at the end of the day, both leave you feeling unsatisfied and wanting more. You are never truly happy with what you have or where you are because you have lost respect for the journey; therefore, you no longer appreciate the ride. If you want to continue progressing as an individual, and especially as an entrepreneur, it is so important that you learn humility. While yes, it is important to be confident in your abilities and to show some level of pride in yourself and what you do, you have to be careful not to get carried away by thinking you are better than others or that you know enough.

Just like everything else in life, it takes balance. You don't want to be so humble that you lose your own self-worth or have a lack of self-esteem, but you don't want to be that prideful person who puts themselves above others either. You have to find that middle ground that keeps you believing in yourself yet still willing to be teachable or submissive when needed. We can't always be in charge of everything, even if life does put us in leadership roles or positions of authority on a regular basis. Even as the boss or owner of a company, there will always be someone who you will have to cater to or submit to in your life. In fact, a lot of people don't realize this, but a business owner usually has more bosses than the employees do. Their customers or clients are their boss because they can choose whether or not they want to do business with them, and any time they are no longer satisfied with the product or service you are providing them, they can fire you by choosing to take their business somewhere else. So you see, as the business owner you have many bosses because you are literally at the mercy of all your customers and your business is dependent upon them. If you don't treat them in a professional and humble manner and you act like you don't need them, then you likely won't stay in business for much longer. Someone who is too prideful will have a very difficult time accepting this concept, but someone who is humble will most likely excel with this way of doing business. Pride will tell you that you don't need to change because your product or service is perfect just the way it is; whereas, humility will tell you that if the customer or client wants it a certain way, then that is what you need to do in order to satisfy the demands and needs of the one who is actually keeping you in business. The prideful person normally refuses to change or admit any fault because they hate being wrong, so they would rather lose a customer and be right than gain a customer and be wrong. On the flip side, a humble person is okay admitting when he or she is wrong. If a potential customer or client wants their product or their service a specific way or at a specific price, a humble business owner will do whatever it takes to cater to their needs because they realize that producing sales is more important than holding onto their pride. So, in reality, when it comes to business, pride can actually cost you money and hold you back from having the type of success that you desire or are capable of having.

So, don't let pride get in the way of holding you back and keeping you from getting to where you want to be in business and in life. Humility, for some, seems to come somewhat naturally while others may have to work a little harder at it, but it is important to have because it is what will keep you centered in life and business. You can't learn if you think you know it all, and you can't grow or overcome if you feel like your way is always the right way. The other scary thing about pride is that the world and life have their own unique way of humbling us when it feels we are getting a little too full of ourselves, and sometimes this can hurt us or cause us to lose a lot of money.

Let me give you an example from my own business experience. By my third year of flipping houses, I started to taste real financial success for the very first time in my young life, and even though I had always considered myself to be pretty humble by nature, this success started to get into my head a little. You see, I have always had the opposite problem, instead of seeing myself as better than others I struggled with self-esteem and always feeling like I wasn't good enough or smart enough. This was especially true when I struggled in school. In fact, in high school I was sometimes called "stupid" or "dumb" because I always seemed to say the wrong thing or was the last one to figure out what was going on around me. I got to the point where I started believing it. Then when I failed to complete my church mission because of clinical depression, failed to complete one semester of college after three attempts, and failed to make it in the cattle business, I was almost convinced that I was not smart enough to achieve financial success. But as I soon discovered what my strengths were as an aspiring entrepreneur and figured out how to apply those strengths, that's when my luck started to change, and so did the way I began to see myself. I started being much more confident and felt like I could do anything I set my mind to. Then once the fruits of my labor started to pay dividends for me, I started to realize that I could go much further than I ever dreamed I could go. After years of self-doubt and failure, it felt really good to finally be successful at something that was important to me, but I started getting a little too overconfident in my ability to make money investing in real estate. I had not only discovered a formula and recipe for success that actually worked in flipping starter homes, but I also found my self-confidence.

After coming off a very successful year of having flipped nine properties and making more money than I ever thought I could, I began thinking that I could do this in my sleep and that success was guaranteed from here on out, but boy, was I in for a reality check. As I mentioned in an earlier chapter, a few flips into my real estate investing career I began purchasing properties that were considered very risky and outside of my basic formula for success I had found in buying starter homes, thinking I could make money in anything. I was so confident in myself that not only did I buy riskier properties, but I started relying on only those properties; I was putting all my eggs in one basket, so to speak. I soon discovered that not every cheap property purchase was the right buy to make. I was having a very difficult time selling properties that year because of the type of houses we had purchased as a company. There was one period when it seemed like nothing was ever going to close and with several hundred-thousand dollars in real estate tied up and no other stream of income I really struggled to stay afloat. I came to realize that success one year does not guarantee success the next, and I could not just buy any old property that looked like a good deal and think I could make easy money on it. Success had gotten the best of me, and after losing a lot of potential profit that year, I finally sold off most of the properties I had purchased, then I had to re-evaluate myself and the business by going back to what had been working, which was buying ranch-style three-bedroom, two-bathroom starter homes. I also decided it was time to bring in new investment strategies, by purchasing long term cash flow rental properties, so my business wasn't so feast or famine. The real estate world truly humbled me and brought me back to reality as I learned that year the importance of not being overconfident or getting too caught up in my own success. Life will humble us from time to time if we don't learn to do it ourselves, and it can be a very painful or expensive lesson to learn if we're not careful.

Another aspect of humility is learning to be selfless enough by passing on what we have figured out in life to others and helping them to succeed as well. To use the knowledge and wisdom we have acquired through our own experiences in order to teach others, so they don't have to learn everything the hard way. Yes, personal experience is the best teacher in life, but there are many trials and hardships we can avoid if we take the time to learn from those who came before us. You can also avoid wasting a lot of time, which is our most precious commodity. Why repeat someone else's painful mistakes if you have the opportunity to learn from theirs? But in order for this to take place, someone has to be willing to teach others through their experiences and pass on what they know or have learned to the next person in line. I feel that is how we have progressed and advanced as a society. I believe that passing down the wisdom and knowledge we have obtained and accumulated is one of the most valuable things you can pass down to someone you care about. Let your experience be a teaching tool for those who are waiting for their turn to pursue their own path or journey to success. If you have already achieved a lot in your lifetime, I am sure that you can pinpoint at least one person who gave you the opportunity to learn from them and helped contribute to your success. So, don't be selfish, pass on what you know, and you will not only be contributing to our society's future, but you will be making a difference in some else's life, probably starting a positive chain reaction of "passing it on." Plus, I have always been a big believer that what goes around, comes around. In other words, if you spread goodness around to others, eventually that same goodness will find its way back to you tenfold.

So, in ending, I want to reemphasize the importance of always staying humble, no matter who you are, where you're from, or what you have accomplished because if you don't, life will remind you of who is really in charge, humbling you and teaching you the hard way. Remember, we are all part of a universe that is much bigger than we are. We are just one tiny piece of the puzzle, which does not at all mean we are of little importance; it just means that the world is so much bigger than ourselves that we owe it our love, respect, and gratitude. If we want the universe to bless us with all it has to offer, then we must be willing to submit ourselves to all it has to teach us by humbling ourselves and abiding by its principles. So, be teachable, always keep an open mind, be willing to change or show flexibility as circumstance requires, be grateful for everything you have been blessed with, and always remember to stay humble. Your personal happiness and your life's pursuit of success depend on it!

NOTES

CONCLUSION

So, now that you have 22 different attributes that you can apply to your own life's pursuit of achieving a successful mindset, what are you going to do about it?

I believe that learning something without applying it to your life is like trying to fly a kite with no wind; the potential within the kite to fly is there, but without the wind there to assist, it's pretty much useless. That is how applying knowledge works—until you put your learning to the test, it will not accomplish anything or do anyone much good. Rather it will sit there in your head waiting for you to put it to use. The same can be said for a tool without the handyman, an instrument without the musician, a ball without the athlete, or a paintbrush without the artist, all are pretty much useless until its counterpart decides to use it in order to make something positive happen. So, while it is very important to learn as much as you can in this life through reading, studying, and listening to others, it is even more important that you take that knowledge and learn to properly apply it in your life. Learn to put it to use so that it serves a purpose for you and everyone in your world, whoever that might be.

These 22 attributes that I have listed and broken down for you, chapter by chapter, have truly guided me my entire life and have been the reason for my success as a real estate investor and entrepreneur. Everything I have done to build up my business to this point in my life I attribute to these very important attributes and principles. I have shared real life personal experiences that have taught me and helped me to grow in ways I needed in order to help shape me into the entrepreneur I am today, and I believe that if I can do it, anyone can. The information I have shared can be applied by anyone no matter where you were born, what your background is, or what your circumstance may be, and I truly believe it is a recipe for success.

The human mind has more power than most people will ever realize, and everything we do or don't do in this life starts with what we choose to feed it and how we choose to use it. Will we feed our mind nutrition, or will we choose to feed it junk? Will we use our minds to improve our own existence and make a difference in the lives of those around us, or will we waste it away by doing only what is convenient and just thinking of ourselves? It's your mind. Decide today what you will feed it and what you will do with it, but know that everything in your world starts and ends with the type of mindset you choose to have. If you want to be happy and successful in this life, then start feeding your mind positive things that will contribute to that state of being. If you want to be miserable and unsuccessful, then only feed it negative things. But who wants to be miserable? Remember, you get out what you choose to put in. So, put good things in your life, and make the choice today to do whatever it takes to have a positive mindset.

Everyone has their own version of what they believe success is to them or how they measure success in their own life. You need to decide what success means to you and where the bar in your own life needs to be set. We are all born into this world with different levels of character, personality, advantage, and expectation; therefore, you cannot reasonably compare yourself to others because it's not fair to them or yourself. God expects us each to be the best version of ourselves, not living up to somebody else's standard. With that being said, I believe that everyone has an equal chance to be great regardless of your background or past choices; you just have to decide to start right where you are and don't stop until you get there. It might take one person longer than another, but that's okay. Life is not a race, but rather it is a test of endurance to see if you have what it takes to endure to the end and be the best you while you're at it. The only limitations you have are the ones you place on yourself, and you are the one who decides what you will do with your time here on Earth and how far you are willing to go.

Wherever you set the bar or the standard for your own life is probably as far as your mind will allow your body to take you, so why not shoot for the stars, and even if you hit the moon, it's better than shooting for the ceiling of your house or not shooting at all, right? Life is about doing your best, not achieving perfection. If you expect to be perfect, then you are destined for a life of disappointment. It might take you several shots or tries, but the amount is not important. What matters most is that you do your best and to never stop trying. That is the true definition of success, to be the best version of yourself and to never give up on your dreams.

So, make the decision right now to create the type of mindset that is going to elevate you to where you want to be in your life and help you to become who you truly want to be deep down inside. Figure out what your definition of success is and develop the mindset to make it happen!

www.ingramcontent.com/pod-product-compliance
Lightning Source LLC
Chambersburg PA
CBHW070535170426
43200CB00011B/2430